THE COMPLETE JAPANESE
ADJECTIVE GUIDE

THE COMPLETE JAPANESE ADJECTIVE GUIDE

BY

ANN TARUMOTO

Tuttle Publishing
Boston • Rutland, Vermont • Tokyo

First published in 2001 by Tuttle Publishing, an imprint of Periplus Editions (HK) Ltd., with editorial offices at 153 Milk Street, Boston, Massachusetts, 02109.

Library of Congress Cataloging-in-Publication Data

Tarumoto, Ann.
   The complete Japanese adjective guide / by Ann Tarumoto.–1st ed.
      p. cm.
  ISBN 0-8048-3276-5 (pbk.)
    1. Japanese language–Adjective. I. Title.

PL577 .T36 2001
495.6'80421–dc21   00-060782

Distributed by

North America, Latin America &
Europe
Tuttle Publishing
Distribution Center
Airport Industrial Park
364 Innovation Drive
North Clarendon, VT 05759-9436
Tel: (802) 773-8930
Toll free tel: (800) 526-2778
Fax: (802) 773-6993
Toll free fax: (800) 329-8885

Japan & Korea
Tuttle Publishing
RK Building, 2nd Floor
2-13-10 Shimo-Meguro, Meguro-Ku
Tokyo 153 0064
Tel: (03) 5437 0171
Fax: (03) 5437 0755

Asia Pacific
Berkeley Books Ltd
5 Little Road #08-01
Cemtex Industrial Bldg
Singapore 536983
Tel: (65) 280-1330
Fax: (65) 280-6290

07 06 05 04 03 02 01   10 9 8 7 6 5 4 3 2 1

Printed in Singapore

CONTENTS

PART II   NA ADJECTIVES

For my parents,
Joe and Kay Imai

INTRODUCTORY NOTES

Keep these two points in mind as you work in this book:

1. *Always VOCALIZE as you do the exercises.* This book is written in
    Romanized Japanese (romaji) to help facilitate visual and oral/aural under-
    standing of the patterns. These exercises were designed to increase your
    familiarity with certain basic adjectives so that you will find yourself being
    able to say them quickly and without stumbling. Hearing yourself say the
    correct response will rapidly increase your aural comprehension of Japanese.

2. *Do all the exercises and complete each exercise.* Even if you think you thoroughly
    understand an inflection or pattern, it is imperative that you start from the
    beginning of the book and do each lesson. The only way you will be able to
    reproduce these patterns in real life conversation is to overlearn them.

GAMBARE !

PART I

ADJECTIVES

1. ADJECTIVES

An adjective is a describing word. To qualify as an adjective in Japanese, a word *must* end in one of the following sounds: **ai, oi, ui, ii**. In Japanese, a word that does not end in one of these sounds is not an adjective and therefore cannot be treated as an adjective, even if it is a describing word.

Memorize this list of adjectives for the exercises to follow.

ii (inflected from yoi)	good
warui	bad
takai	expensive, high, tall (in position)
yasui	inexpensive
chikai	near
tooi	far
atsui	hot
samui	cold (weather only)
oishii	delicious, tasty
mazui	bad-tasting
ookii	large, big
chiisai	small, little
muzukashii	difficult
yasashii	easy, nice (people)
suzushii	cool (weather)
atatakai (attakai)	warm (weather, clothing, people)
atsui	hot (objects, weather)
tsumetai	cold (objects, personalities)
furui	old (not for people)
atarashii	new (objects, people)

hayai	early, fast
osoi	late, slow

amai	sweet (tasting)
karai	salty, spicy

omoshiroi	interesting
tanoshii	fun
isogashii	busy

Write the antonym of each adjective:

1. samui _____

2. tsumetai _____

3. furui _____

4. hayai _____

5. chiisai _____

6. ii _____

7. yasui _____

8. tooi _____

9. atsui _____

10. osoi _____

11. yasashii _____

12. mazui _____

13. takai _____

14. ookii _____

15. atarashii _____

16. warui _____

17. chikai _____

18. muzukashii _____

19. oishii _____

20. amai _____

What would be an appropriate adjective to describe the following?

1. a two-karat diamond _____

2. a school 50 miles from your house _____

3. an office worker with no time for lunch _____

4. a calculus problem _____

5. a meal at the best restaurant _____

6. a perfect grade on an exam _____

7. a day at an amusement park _____

8. an elephant _____

9. a month-old loaf of bread _____

10. a jalapeño pepper _____

11. a train that travels 75 mph _____

12. a mouse _____

2. ADJECTIVES MODIFYING NOUNS

In Japanese, as in English, an adjective often modifies or describes a *noun*. Like English, when an adjective modifies a noun, it precedes the noun directly, *without* an intervening *particle*.

> Example: omoshiroi hon = an interesting book

Describe the word **kuruma** (car) with the adjective indicated.

1. _____ kuruma
   old

2. _____ kuruma
   expensive

3. _____ kuruma
   big

Try expressing the following phrases. Look up the nouns you don't know in the glossary:

1. an inexpensive car =

   _____

2. a new TV =

   _____

3. an interesting movie =

   _____

4. hot coffee =

   _____

5. a cold drink =

   _____

6. a warm day =

   _____

7. fresh vegetables =

   _____

8. an old radio =

_____

9. a busy day =

_____

10. a cold person =

_____

11. a large dog =

_____

12. a small cat =

_____

13. a faraway place =

_____

14. an expensive sweater =

_____

15. a good book =

_____

By adding **desu** or one of its forms after the *noun* you can make a simple sentence. The forms of **desu** are:

desu (present)	ja arimasen (present negative)
deshita (past)	ja arimasen deshita (past negative)

Example: Ii hon desu ka?   = Is it a good book?
           Ii hon ja arimasen deshita. = It wasn't a good book.

Try these in Japanese:

1. It was an interesting movie.

_____

2. It isn't delicious sushi.

_____

3. It was hot coffee.

_____

4. Is it a good book?

_____

5. It wasn't a new TV.

_____

6. It was a good school.

_____

7. It's a restaurant that is nearby.

   _____

8. It wasn't a big cat.

   _____

9. It isn't a small dog.

   _____

10. It was a difficult problem.

    _____

11. It's not a large post office.

    _____

12. It's not an expensive department store.

    _____

3. WHEN ADJECTIVES ARE USED IN THE PREDICATE

The adjectives listed in the beginning of this workbook are in what is known as their *dictionary form.* Adjectives in their dictionary form are complete sentences. The addition of **desu** to the end of an adjective will make the sentence more polite. However, it will not change the meaning of the sentence, and it will not make the sentence more grammatically correct.

The following sentences are in what could be called the *non-past tense.* This means that the tense of the sentence can be either *present* or *future* but *not* the past. Therefore:

> Rajio ga ii. / Rajio ga ii desu. = The radio is good. / The radio will be good.

How would you say these sentences more politely?

1. Sono rajio wa ii.

    _____

2. Ano biiru wa oishii.

    _____

3. Gakkoo wa chikai.

    _____

4. Kyoo wa isogashii.

    _____

5. Kono terebi wa ookii.

    _____

6. Ano sakana wa furui.

    _____

7. Ano sushi wa mazui.

    _____

8. Hikooki wa hayai.

    _____

9. Tempura wa yasui.

    _____

10. Sensei wa yasashii.

    _____

Tell your teacher (politely) that:

1. It is hot. _____

2. You are busy. _____

3. It is difficult. _____

4. It is cool. _____

5. Japanese is easy. _____

Tell a good friend (no need to be polite!) that:

1. It is warm. _____

2. The coffee is hot. _____

3. The car is new. _____

4. The restaurant is expensive. _____

5. The vegetables are fresh. _____

Fill in the missing syllables in these adjectives:

1. to___i	2. chii___I	3. ___okii	4. ya___shii
5. ta___i	6. ___zukashii	7. ya___i	8. ta___shii
9. a___i	10. i___gashii	11. chi___sai	12. fu___i
13. ata___kai	14. ___tsui	15. a___rashii	16. ___i
17. ka___i	18. ___yai	19. ma___i	20. ___ishii

ADJECTIVES IN A NEGATIVE PREDICATE (NON-PAST)

When you want to express a sentence such as, "The dog is not *big*," the adjective in Japanese appears in the predicate of the sentence. It is also in its *negative* form. To inflect an adjective to its negative form in the non-past tense, drop the last **i** and add **-ku arimasen.**

Example: Samui desu. (It is cold.) > Samuku arimasen. (It is not cold.)

Samuku arimasen is the most formal way of expressing the idea, *It is not cold.*

The only exception to this rule is **ii** (good). Remember that **ii** is inflected from **yoi.** Therefore, **ii desu** means *it is good* while **yoku arimasen** means *it is not good.*

Inflect these adjectives to their *formal, negative, non-past* forms:

1. atarashii desu _____

2. ii desu _____

3. isogashii desu _____

4. furui desu _____

5. hayai desu _____

6. amai desu _____

7. tanoshii desu _____

8. omoshiroi desu _____

9. takai desu _____

10. yasui desu _____

11. muzukashii desu _____

12. ookii desu _____

13. tooi desu _____

14. warui desu _____

15. mazui desu _____

Answer *no* to all these questions using the negative form of the adjective:

1. Ano inu wa ookii desu ka?
   Iie. _____

2. Daigaku wa chikai desu ka?
   Iie. _____

3. Kono hon wa omoshiroi desu ka?
   Iie. _____

4. Nihongo wa muzukashii desu ka?
   Iie. _____

5. Kuruma wa atarashii desu ka?
   Iie. _____

6. Ano sensei wa ii desu ka?
   Iie. _____

7. Sushi wa mazui desu ka?
   Iie. _____

8. Kyoo wa atsui desu ka?
   Iie. _____

9. Juusu wa tsumetai desu ka?
   Iie. _____

10. Karee raisu wa karai desu ka?
    Iie. _____

Compose the following sentences using the *negative, formal non-past* form of the appropriate adjective. Keep in mind that subject pronouns such as *I, you, he, she, it,* and *they* need *not* be translated in Japanese. Although there is no word for *the* in Japanese, you may use the word **sono** where *the* appears.

1. It is not hot. _____

2. He is not busy. _____

3. The coffee is not cold. _____

4. The car is not new. _____

5. The juice is not sweet. _____

6. The tempura is not good. _____

7. The magazine is not good. _____

8. The vegetables are not fresh. _____

9. The problem is not difficult. _____

10. The school is not far. _____

11. The dog is not large. _____

12. The movie is not interesting. _____

NEGATIVE ADJECTIVES IN THE PREDICATE: THE PLAIN FORM

We have been working with the *formal* forms of adjectives in the non-past. It is also possible to express the same ideas using the *plain* or *informal, negative* form of adjectives. This "friendly" way of speaking comes from replacing **arimasen** with **nai.**

Example: Samuku arimasen. > Samuku nai.

Both these sentences mean "It is not cold." **Samuku nai** is merely a more friendly or direct way of expressing this idea.

Give the *plain* form of the following *formal* sentences and explain what they mean:

1. Omoshiroku arimasen.

   _____

2. Kore wa atarashiku arimasen.

   _____

3. Kono zasshi wa waruku arimasen.

   _____

4. Kono koohii wa atsuku arimasen.

   _____

5. Ano kuruma wa furuku arimasen.

   _____

Write the *plain negative* forms of the following sentences:

1. Ano neko wa ookii.

   _____

2. Shiken wa muzukashii.

   _____

3. Uchi wa chiisai.

   _____

4. Kyoo wa suzushii.

   _____

5. Kono seetaa wa atatakai.

   _____

6. Fuyu wa samui.

   _____

7. Piza wa mazui.

   _____

8. Ano hon wa ii.

   _____

9. Nihon wa tooi.

   _____

10. Kyoo wa tanoshii.

    _____

Compose these sentences using the *plain negative* form of the appropriate adjectives. Use **sono** for *the*.

1. The soup is not hot.

   _____

2. The house is not big.

   _____

3. Today is not hot.

   _____

4. The magazine isn't interesting.

   _____

5. The explanation isn't difficult.

   _____

6. The teacher isn't nice.

   _____

7. The dictionary isn't good.

   _____

8. Today isn't warm.

   _____

9. The TV isn't new.

   _____

10. The station isn't far.

    _____

11. Japan isn't near.

    _____

12. The tickets are not expensive.

    _____

ADJECTIVES IN THE PREDICATE: THE PAST AFFIRMATIVE

Adjectives in Japanese must be inflected to their past tense. You cannot simply take the non-past formal form **samui desu** and change **desu** to **deshita**. Adjectives are made past tense by dropping the last **i** and replacing it with **-katta.**

    Example: samui > samukatta

Samukatta is the plain past tense. It means, *It was cold.* The addition of **desu,** as in **samukatta desu,** makes the sentence more formal, but does not alter the meaning in any way.

Remember that **ii** is always inflected from **yoi.**

Change these adjectives in the plain affirmative non-past to the *plain affirmative past tense* and give the English equivalent:

Example: warui > Warukatta. = It was bad.

1. attakai >

   _____

2. karai >

   _____

3. tanoshii >

   _____

4. ookii >

   _____

5. muzukashii >

   _____

6. takai >

   _____

7. yasashii >

   _____

8. amai >

   _____

9. isogashii >

   _____

10. suzushii >

   _____

Change these sentences to the *formal past* tense:

1. Ano mondai wa yasashii desu.

   _____

2. Ano suupu wa atsui desu.

   _____

3. Kyoo wa suzushii desu.

   _____

4. Sensei wa ii desu.

   _____

5. Setsumei wa warui desu.

   _____

6. Nihon no jisho wa takai desu.

   _____

7. Piza wa mazui desu.

   _____

8. Seetaa wa atatakai desu.

   _____

9. Yuubinkyoku wa tooi desu.

   _____

10. Zasshi wa omoshiroi desu.

    _____

Change these sentences as indicated by the word in parentheses:

   Example: Kyoo wa atsui desu. (kinoo) > Kinoo wa atsukatta desu.

1. Kinoo wa samukatta desu. (kyoo) _____

2. Ashita wa isogashii desu. (ototoi) _____

3. Kyoo wa samui desu. (kyonen) _____

4. Kyoo no tempura wa oishii desu. (kinoo no tempura)

   _____

5. Senshuu wa tanoshikatta desu. (ima) _____

How do you say these sentences in Japanese? Be sure to make the distinction between past and non-past sentences. Use **sono** to indicate *the*.

1. The pizza was cold. _____

2. The school is large. _____

3. The books are inexpensive. _____

4. The sweater was warm. _____

5. Yesterday was fun. _____

6. The soup is cold. _____

7. Today was cool. _____

8. The girl is small. _____

9. The post office is far. _____

10. The problems were difficult. _____

11. Games are fun. _____

12. The teacher was nice. _____

13. The sushi was expensive. _____

14. Saturday was hot. _____

15. The explanation was good. _____

16. The newspaper is old. _____

17. The movie was interesting. _____

18. The vegetables are fresh. _____

19. Planes are fast. _____

20. The TV was expensive. _____

ADJECTIVES IN THE PREDICATE: THE PAST NEGATIVE

If you want to express the idea *It was not cold* in Japanese, you must change the adjective *samui* into its *past negative* form, **Samuku arimasen deshita.** This tense is formed by dropping the last **i** from the adjective and adding **-ku arimasen deshita.** The resulting past negative form is *formal*.

Change the following adjectives to their *formal past negative* forms and tell what they mean in English:

1. tanoshii > _____

2. oishii > _____

3. atatakai > _____

4. karai > _____

5. ookii > _____

6. muzukashii > _____

7. tooi > _____

8. ii > _____

9. amai > _____

10. suzushii > _____

What do these sentences mean in English?

1. Densha wa hayaku arimasen deshita.
   _____

2. Ano konpyuuta wa yoku arimasen deshita.
   _____

3. Kyoo wa suzushikatta desu.
   _____

4. Sono rajio wa yasuku arimasen deshita.
   _____

5. Amerika no zasshi wa omoshiroku arimasen.
   _____

6. Sono sakana wa furukatta desu.
   _____

7. Sono kudamono wa amaku arimasen deshita.
   _____

8. Kono kuruma wa chiisaku arimasen.
   _____

9. Ano niku wa atarashiku arimasen deshita.
   _____

10. Kono kooto wa atatakaku arimasen.

_____

Now, try composing the following sentences using the *formal past negative* form of the appropriate adjective:

1. It wasn't cold yesterday. _____

2. The tea wasn't hot. _____

3. The water wasn't cold. _____

4. I wasn't busy. _____

5. The TV show wasn't interesting. _____

6. The sushi wasn't good. _____

7. The restaurant wasn't expensive. _____

8. The train wasn't late. _____

9. The newspapers weren't old. _____

10. The house wasn't large. _____

11. The weather wasn't bad. _____

12. The explanation wasn't difficult. _____

13. The school wasn't nearby. _____

14. The cat wasn't small. _____

15. The store wasn't inexpensive. _____

16. The TV wasn't big. _____

17. The room wasn't cool. _____

18. The bus wasn't early. _____

19. The pizza wasn't bad tasting. _____

20. It wasn't fun yesterday. _____

THE PAST NEGATIVE: PLAIN FORM

As with the other forms we have studied so far, the negative past tense has a *plain* form as well as a *formal* form. The *plain* form may be obtained by replacing **arimasen deshita** with **nakatta.** Therefore, the equivalent *plain* form of **samuku arimasen deshita** (it is not cold) is **samuku nakatta.**

Change these *formal* sentences to a *plain* form and give the English equivalent:

1. Oishiku arimasen deshita. > _____
   (Eng.) _____
2. Ookiku arimasen deshita. > _____
   _____
3. Inu wa chiisaku arimasen deshita. > _____
   _____
4. Amerika no eiga wa omoshiroku arimasen deshita. > ____
   _____
5. Tenki wa yoku arimasen deshita. > _____
   _____
6. Kono karee wa karaku arimasen deshita. > _____
   _____
7. Mondai wa muzukashiku arimasen deshita. > _____
   _____
8. Suupu wa atsuku arimasen deshita. > _____
   _____
9. Kyoo wa suzushiku arimasen deshita. > _____
   _____
10. Yuubinkyoku wa tooku arimasen deshita. > _____
    _____
11. Niku wa atarashiku arimasen deshita. > _____
    _____
12. Yasai wa yasuku arimasen deshita. > _____
    _____

Try composing the following sentences using the *plain* form of the appropriate adjective:

1. The coffee wasn't hot. _____

2. The newspaper wasn't expensive. _____

3. The teacher wasn't good. _____

4. Today wasn't warm. _____

5. The dictionary wasn't cheap. _____

6. The post office wasn't far. _____

7. School wasn't fun. _____

8. The bread wasn't fresh. _____

9. The car wasn't fast. _____

10. The Coke wasn't cold. _____

11. The computer wasn't old. _____

12. The weather wasn't bad. _____

4. ZENZEN, TOKIDOKI AND OTHER ADVERBS

Adjectives can be described by adverbs such as **totemo, tokidoki** and **zenzen.**

The following adverbs can only be used with an *affirmative* predicate (past & non-past).

Adverb	Meaning
tokidoki	sometimes
totemo	very, a lot
itsumo	always
kanari	quite
chotto	a little

The following adverbs can only be used with a *negative* predicate (past & non-past).

Adverb	Meaning
zenzen	not at all, never, in no way
amari, anmari	not very

The following adverb can be used with *either* affirmative or negative predicates.

Adverb	Meaning
taitei	usually

Adverbs are usually placed directly *before* the adjectives they modify.

Example: Totemo omoshiroi desu. = It is very interesting.
Ano eiga wa anmari omoshiroku nai. = That movie is not very interesting.

Don't make the mistake in thinking that **zenzen** and **amari** with a negative predicate constitute a double negative. Those adverbs by themselves will not make a negative sentence. The sentence is not negative until the predicate is put in negative form.

Try this exercise. You may use either formal or plain forms of the adjective.

1. It is very interesting. _____

2. I'm not busy at all. _____

3. It doesn't taste very good. _____

4. It's always fun. _____

5. It's not hot at all. _____

6. Sometimes it's expensive. _____

7. It's not difficult at all. _____

8. It's usually cool. _____

9. It's quite warm. _____

10. It wasn't very early. _____

11. Sometimes they're cheap. _____

12. I was very busy. _____

13. It's not very easy. _____

14. It was quite far. _____

15. Sometimes it's good. _____

16. It was quite bad. _____

17. It's always good. _____

18. It's not very old. _____

19. They're quite new. _____

20. It's not at all interesting. _____

21. It's a little large. _____

22. It's quite cold. _____

23. It was always expensive. _____

24. It was a little old. _____

25. I wasn't busy at all. _____

There are many adverbs in Japanese other than the ones presented here. When you come across a new one, find out whether it can be used with only affirmative, only negative, or both types of sentences.

5. OTHER ADJECTIVES

If you have completed all the exercises so far, you are probably an expert at changing adjectives to the negative present, the past tense and the negative past tense. The manner in which you have changed the adjectives listed so far in this workbook is the *same for any adjective* in Japanese. Following is a list of some other adjectives in Japanese. By following the rules you have mastered in the previous pages, you should be able to handle the exercises without any difficulty.

abunai	=	dangerous
akai	=	red
aoi	=	blue
itai	=	painful
kawaii	=	cute (objects, people, animals)
kibishii	=	strict
kitanai	=	dirty
kowai	=	scary
kuroi	=	black
kuwashii	=	detailed
mazushii	=	poor (economic status)
mezurashii	=	unusual
mushiatsui	=	hot and humid
sabishii	=	lonely
shiroi	=	white
subarashii	=	fantastic
sugoi	=	awesome
tsuyoi	=	strong
ureshii	=	happy
urusai	=	noisy, annoying
utsukushii	=	beautiful
wakai	=	young

Now, referring to the list above, see if you can figure out what the following sentences mean. Look up any new nouns in the glossary.

1. Watashi no Nihongo no sensei wa kibishii desu.

2. Sugokatta!

3. Kuruma wa akakatta desu.

4. Tookyoo no natsu wa totemo mushiatsui desu.

5. Haha wa wakaku arimasen.

6. Setsumei wa zenzen kuwashiku nakatta.

7. Ano inu wa kowaku arimasen.

8. Kyoo no tenki wa subarashikatta desu.

9. Heya wa anmari kitanaku nai.

10. Atama wa itaku nakatta.

11. Ano chiimu wa totemo tsuyoi desu.

12. Kore wa mezurashii okashi desu ne.

13. Sora wa aoi desu ka?

14. Ano michi wa abunakatta.

15. Kabe wa shiroku arimasen deshita.

Answer *no* to these questions:

1. Kuruma wa kuroi desu ka?
   Iie. _____

2. Kinoo wa mushiatsukatta desu ka?
   Iie. _____

3. Nihon no o-cha wa mezurashii desu ka?
   Iie. _____

4. Atama wa itakatta desu ka?
   Iie. _____

5. Anata wa ima ureshii desu ka?
   Iie. _____

Try making your own sentences using the following words. Use as many of the forms studied as possible.

Example: kyoo—samui   Kyoo wa samuku arimasen.

1. neko—kawaii
   _____

2. tenki—warui
   _____

3. kuruma—abunai
   _____

4. keshiki—subarashii
   _____

5. toire—kitanai
   _____

Try changing these adjectives as indicated by the English sentence. Use the *formal* form.

1. It was very dirty. _____

2. I'm not happy. _____

3. He was cute. _____

4. I wasn't lonely. _____

5. It's not dangerous. _____

6. It was red. _____

Do the same for the following, but use the *plain* form:

1. Awesome! _____

2. It's not unusual. _____

3. It wasn't blue. _____

4. It was quite detailed. _____

5. She isn't strict at all. _____

6. THE GOLDILOCKS LEVEL AND THE NEGATIVE

As you learned previously, it is possible to form both formal and informal levels in both the past and non-past tenses in Japanese. However, in both the *negative past* and the *negative non-past*, it is possible to create an intermediate level between the formal and informal levels. I like to call this the Goldilocks level as it is neither too formal nor too informal. For most occasions, it is just right. This level is only applicable for adjectives in their negative form.

The Goldilocks level is simply gotten by adding the word **desu** to the plain form of the negative adjective. This is done in both the past and non-past tenses. In this use, the word **desu** is *never* changed to **deshita** in the past.

> Example: *atsuku nai* becomes *atsuku nai desu.*
> *atsuku nakatta* becomes *atsuku nakatta desu.*

The meanings of **atsuku nai, atsuku arimasen, atsuku nai desu** are the same, i.e., *it is not hot.* The only difference is the level of formality.

Let's work on the *negative* of the non-past. Give the levels indicated for each adjective:

> Example: tooi
> Formal   Tooku arimasen.
> Plain   Tooku nai.
> Goldilocks   Tooku nai desu.
> English   It is not far.

1. samui
   Formal _____
   Plain _____
   Goldilocks _____
   English _____

2. tanoshii
Formal _____
Plain _____
Goldilocks _____
English _____

3. amai
Formal _____
Plain _____
Goldilocks _____
English _____

4. atatakai
Formal _____
Plain _____
Goldilocks _____
English _____

5. osoi
Formal _____
Plain _____
Goldilocks _____
English _____

Now try the past negative:

1. muzukashii
Formal _____
Plain _____
Goldilocks _____
English _____

2. chikai
Formal _____
Plain _____
Goldilocks _____
English _____

3. isogashii
   Formal _____
   Plain _____
   Goldilocks _____
   English _____

4. ii
   Formal _____
   Plain _____
   Goldilocks _____
   English _____

5. akai (red)
   Formal _____
   Plain _____
   Goldilocks _____
   English _____

Goldilocks is a level often used by the Japanese in conversation, as it is polite without stuffiness, and friendly without rudeness.

To summarize, there are two levels of speech in the affirmative, both past and non-past, (*formal* and *plain*), and there are three levels in the negative (formal, informal, and Goldilocks).

7. DESHOO AND DESHOO?

The addition of **deshoo** to an adjective in either the affirmative or negative, past or non-past, can have one of two meanings. When it is said with a rising intonation **deshoo?** it carries the meaning of *isn't it? aren't they? aren't you?* etc. This **deshoo?** corresponds roughly to **desu ne,** although **deshoo?** is somewhat less certain than **desu ne.** Thus, **samui deshoo?** and **samui desu ne** both mean, *it's cold, isn't it?*

When **deshoo** is said with a lowering intonation, it takes on the meaning of *probably, must be, must not be, must have been,* or *must not have been,* depending on the tense of the adjective. This **deshoo** is often used by the Japanese when speaking of the states of being and the emotions of others. For example, the Japanese would never point to someone and say, "Samui desu" (she feels cold). They would rather say, **Samui deshoo** (she probably feels cold, or she must be cold), as they cannot state with certainty the condition of another person.

The difference in intonation is best studied orally. Our purpose here is to understand its usage and practice its formation.

For both usages, the word **deshoo** is added to the plain form of the adjective in the non-past affirmative and negative, and in the past affirmative and negative. **Deshoo** requires that a *plain* form precede it. However, the resulting sentence is considered *formal.*

Example:	Oishii deshoo.	=	It probably tastes good.
	Oishiku nai deshoo?	=	It doesn't taste good, does it?
	Oishikatta deshoo?	=	It was good, wasn't it?
	Oishiku nakatta deshoo.	=	It must not have tasted good.

In this exercise, read the description of the situation and respond with an appropriate form of **oishii** and either **deshoo** or **deshoo?** Think carefully about the tense of your sentences.

1. You've brought your friend to your favorite Tex-Mex restaurant. Your friend wants to order a new dish on the menu, guacamole sushi. You discourage him by saying:

2. The two of you select the specialty tacos. Your food arrives and as you eat, you say to your friend:

_____

3. You look at the dessert menu and your friend asks how the caramel flan is. You say you've never tried it, but:

_____

4. Your meal was superb. Your friend has just licked the last of the caramel flan off his plate. You say:

_____

5. Your friend recounts his last experience with a Tex-Mex meal at the Grungy Gerry's Taco Palace. You say:

_____

Read these sentences aloud with the proper intonaton and then explain what they mean. An asterisk next to an adjective means that you will find the meaning in the Other Adjectives section of this text.

1. Kyoo wa suzushii deshoo?

_____

2. Ashita mo suzushii deshoo.

_____

3. Ano eiga wa omoshiroku nakatta deshoo?

_____

4. Nihon wa utsukushii deshoo.

_____

5. Nihongo wa muzukashiku nai deshoo?

_____

6. Kono mizu wa tsumetai deshoo?

_____

7. Tookyoo wa mushiatsukatta* deshoo.

_____

8. Sugoi* deshoo?!

_____

9. Ima wa isogashiku nai deshoo.

_____

10. Hikooki wa hayai deshoo?

_____

Using the adjective indicated, write the Japanese equivalent of the following sentences. As you write, vocalize your answers with the proper intonation. Also keep in mind that subject pronouns such as *it, they, he,* etc. are usually not used in Japanese.

Be careful with your tenses! *Must have been* and *must not have been* indicate situations in the past.

1. yasashii
   It's probably easy. _____
   It must have been easy. _____
   It wasn't easy, was it? _____

2. mushiatsui
   It must be hot & humid. _____
   It was hot & humid, wasn't it? _____
   It probably isn't hot & humid. _____

3. omoshiroi
   It isn't interesting, is it? _____
   It's probably not interesting. _____
   It must be interesting. _____

4. mazushii
   They're probably poor. _____
   They're poor, aren't they? _____
   They're not poor, are they? _____

5. kibishii
   She was strict, wasn't she? _____
   She's probably not strict. _____
   She's strict, isn't she? _____

6. ureshii
   She must be happy. _____
   She's probably not happy. _____
   She must have been happy. _____

7. sabishii
   He must be lonely. _____
   He must have been lonely. _____
   He probably wasn't lonely. _____

8. shiroi
   It's white, isn't it? _____
   It wasn't white, was it? _____
   It must have been white. _____

Read these situations. Select an appropriate adjective and add either **deshoo** or **deshoo?** Again, be careful of the tense you use. Refer to the Other Adjectives list if you need help.

1. You heard that Taroo has a new girlfriend. You're with him when he gets a perfumed letter from her. He is all smiles. You say to him:

   _____

2. The organic chemistry course at your university has a reputation for being tough. When you are asked by a freshman about the rigor of the professors, you say:

   _____

3. You and your friend are monster movie aficionados. After seeing the latest box office hit in this genre, you say to her:

   _____

4. You bump into a friend on his way to get a flu shot. You allay his fears about the pain of the injection by saying:

   _____

5. Although you've never visited Alaska in mid-January, what comment could you reasonably make about the weather at that time of year?

   _____

6. Your friends are discussing Hanako's new 2-carat engagement ring. What comment could you make about its price?

   _____

7. Toshio tells you that earlier that day, he played 5 sets of tennis when the temperature was 95 degrees in the shade. What would be an appropriate verbal reaction on your part?

_____

8. What comment could be made about the volume of business in June at a store specializing in skiing equipment?

_____

8. STRADDLING THE FENCE

Very often you will hear the particle **wa** inserted between the **-ku** form and any negative form. Look at this brief exchange:

> Q: Kono terebi **wa** takakatta desu ka?
> A: Iie. Takaku **wa** nakatta desu.

In response to the question, *Was this TV expensive?* the speaker answers, *No. It wasn't what one would call expensive.* The speaker's answer does not mean, however, that the TV was *inexpensive.* The **wa** particle in this case is used to "straddle the fence" as the speaker wants to say that although the item in question was *not* expensive, he does not want to go so far as to say that it was cheap.

Other ways to think of this pattern in English would be:

> It's not exactly what you'd call expensive.
> I wouldn't say that it was expensive.

This construction may be used with any negative form:

> atsuku wa arimasen
> atsuku wa nai desu
> atsuku wa nai
>
> atsuku wa arimasen deshita
> atsuku wa nakatta desu
> atsuku wa nakatta

Answer these questions using the **wa** particle to "qualify" the negative. It is not necessary to repeat the subject if it is understood. Give the English equivalent of your answer.

1. Kono terebi wa ii desu ne. Takakatta desu ka?
   Iie. _____
   (Eng.) _____

2. Sono suupu wa oishii desu ka?
   Iie. _____
   _____

3. Nihongo wa muzukashii desu ka?
   Iie. _____
   _____

4. Sono shoosetsu wa omoshiroi desu ka?
   Iie. _____
   _____

5. Kyoo wa isogashikatta desu ka?
   Iie. _____
   _____

6. Natsu wa atsukatta desu ka?
   Iie. _____
   _____

7. Anata no uchi wa hiroi desu ka?
   Iie. _____
   _____

8. Mizu wa tsumetai deshoo?
   Iie. _____
   _____

9. Yama wa tooi deshoo?
   Iie. _____
   _____

10. Sono sensei wa warui desu ka?
    Iie. _____
    _____

11. Kono suupaa no yasai wa atarashii deshoo?
    Iie. _____
    _____

12. Sono depaato wa yasui desu ka?
    Iie. _____

    _____

13. Sono eiga wa omoshirokatta deshoo?
    Iie. _____

    _____

14. Kono jisho wa furui desu ka?
    Iie. _____

    _____

15. Sono basu wa hayakatta deshoo?
    Iie. _____

    _____

9. Soo Desu

The use of **soo desu** following the *plain* form of an adjective differs from the **soo desu** meaning *it's true, that's correct,* etc. The **soo desu** we are going to look at here is used to report hearsay as in, *I understand that it . . . , I hear that . . . , I heard that. . . .*

This construction is made by adding **soo desu** to a *plain* form of the adjective in both the *past, non-past, affirmative,* and *negative* depending on what you want your sentence to mean.

Example:	Samui soo *desu.*	=	I understand it *is* cold.
	Samuku nai soo *desu.*	=	I understand it *isn't* cold.
	Samukatta soo *desu.*	=	I understand it *was* cold.
	Samuku nakatta soo *desu.*	=	I understand it *wasn't* cold.

Notice that **desu** is *not* changed to the *past* or *negative.* Those issues have already been taken care of by the adjective preceding **soo desu.** The use of the *plain* form is a requirement before **soo desu** and does not mean that the sentence is *informal.*

Write the meaning of the following in Japanese. Do not translate subject pronouns such as *I, she, he, they, it,* etc.

1. I hear it's hot.

   _____

   I hear it's not hot.

   _____

   I hear it was hot.

   _____

   I hear it wasn't hot.

   _____

2. I understand that she's busy.

   _____

   I understand that she was busy.

   _____

I understand that she wasn't busy.

_____

I understand that she isn't busy.

_____

3. It's my understanding that it's new.

_____

It's my understanding that it wasn't new.

_____

It's my understanding that it's not new.

_____

It's my understanding that it was new.

_____

4. I heard that it's expensive.

_____

I heard that it's not expensive.

_____

I heard that it wasn't expensive.

_____

I heard that it was expensive.

_____

5. I understand that it wasn't good.

_____

I understand that it's not good.

_____

I understand that it was good.

_____

I understand that it is good.

_____

What do you think these sentences mean?

1. Ano resutoran wa totemo oishii soo desu.

_____

2. Sono zasshi wa zenzen omoshiroku nakatta soo desu.

_____

3. Shiken wa totemo muzukashii soo desu.

_____

4. Ano kutsu wa anmari yoku nai soo desu.

   _____

5. Tenki wa ii soo desu.

   _____

6. Eiga no kippu wa yasukatta soo desu.

   _____

Now it's your turn to try your hand at making sentences with **soo desu.**

1. I understand that she's *very* busy today.

   _____

2. My understanding is that it will cost a lot.

   _____

3. I heard that the tickets weren't cheap.

   _____

4. I heard that Japan isn't *very* hot.

   _____

5. I hear that her house isn't *very* big.

   _____

6. I heard that the test wasn't difficult *at all.*

   _____

7. I understand that the vegetables aren't *very* fresh.

   _____

8. I heard that the car was old.

   _____

9. I heard that it was *a lot of* fun.

   _____

10. I hear that the train isn't *very* fast.

    _____

10. THE -KU FORM OF THE ADJECTIVE

When an adjective in Japanese is used to describe the *way an action is done,* the adjective must be changed to its **-ku** form. In other words, the **-ku** form is the adverb form of the adjective. This form is already familiar to you in the negative form of adjectives. Here, let's look at other ways in which the **-ku** form is used.

The **-ku** form or adverb form of an adjective is made by dropping the last **i** from the dictionary form and adding **-ku.** Thus, **atsui** becomes **atsuku.** The only exception to this is the adjective **ii** which is always inflected from **yoi.** The adverb form of **ii** is **yoku.** (The adverb **yoku,** by the way, can mean *well, often, a great deal.*)

Write the **-ku** form of the following adjectives:

1. atsui _____

2. omoshiroi _____

3. kibishii* _____

4. amai _____

5. hayai _____

6. isogashii _____

7. tanoshii _____

8. akai* _____

9. mazushii* _____

10. tooi _____

11. ookii _____

12. yasui _____

13. ii _____

14. chikai _____

15. suzushii _____

16. yasashii _____

17. karai _____

18. oishii _____

19. atarashii _____

20. warui _____

The word **narimashita** is the past tense of the verb **narimasu**, meaning *become.* In colloquial English, we sometimes use the word *get* for **narimasu** or *got* for **narimashita** as in *It got (became) hot.* In Japanese we would say **atsuku narimashita.** The **-ku** form of the adjective is used, as it describes *how* something became.

Write the following sentences using the **-ku** form of the appropriate adjectives with either **narimasu** or **narimashita** depending on the tense of the English sentence. Keep in mind that **narimasu** is used for both present and future situations.

1. It got cold. _____

2. It became cheap(er). _____

3. It got interesting. _____

4. It will get easy. _____

5. It became red. _____

6. It gets fun. _____

7. She became beautiful. _____

8. We got busy. _____

9. She got well. _____

10. It will get dirty. _____

11. It will get cool. _____

12. It got noisy. _____

13. Japanese became difficult. _____

14. The teacher became strict. _____

15. The problem became easy. _____

16. The car became old. _____

17. It will get warm. _____

18. The weather got bad. _____

19. The coffee became cold. _____

20. I became lonely. _____

The **-ku** form is also used with the verb **shimasu** to express the idea someone *makes* something big, small, cheap, etc.

    Example: She will make it large. = Ookiku shimasu.
                       She made it large.   = Ookiku shimashita.

Since the adjective describes *how* someone does something, the **-ku** form of the adjective is required.

Try this exercise. Again, take care to choose the proper tense of the verb **shimasu**.

1. I'll make it hot. _____

2. He lowered the price._____

3. They made it interesting. _____

4. I'll make it early. _____

5. The teacher made it difficult. _____

6. Will you make them small? _____

7. He made it fun. _____

8. She made it spicy. _____

The following is a list of verbs with their English eguivalents. Although each verb here is given in the past tense, the **-ku** form of the adjective may be used with any tense.

tabemashita	ate
kaimashita	bought
arukimashita	walked
kimashita	came
benkyoo shimashita	studied
hatarakimashita	worked
oshiemashita	taught
tatemashita	built
asobimashita	played
urimashita	sold
setsumei shimashita	explained
okimashita	woke up
nemashita	went to bed
iimashita	said
hanashimashita	spoke, talked

See if you can understand the meaning of the sentences below. If you get stumped, start with the verb and work backwards. If the subject or object of the sentence has been omitted in the Japanese sentence, supply an appropriate one. Keep in mind that although a literal translation may not work sometimes, the **-ku** form of the adjective will always describe *how* an action is done.

Example: Kuwashiku setsumei shimashita.
           Literally: [She] explained [it] detailedly.
           Better: [She] explained [it] in detail.

1. Hayaku okimashita. _____

2. Osoku kimashita. _____

3. Isogashiku hatarakimashita. _____

4. Kuruma o takaku urimashita. _____

5. Sensei wa kibishiku oshiemashita. _____

6. Hayaku nemashita. _____

7. Uchi o atarashiku tatemashita. _____

8. Sensei wa kuwashiku setsumei shimashita. _____
    _____

Translate the following sentences. The sentences are in idiomatic English, but can be said using one of the adjectives you already know.

1. I sold it at a low price. _____

2. We came late. _____

3. She went to sleep early. _____

4. He spoke in detail. _____

5. She said it nicely. _____

6. He studied well. _____

7. I bought it at a high price. _____

8. They played merrily. _____

9. I told her sternly. _____

10. We got up late. _____

11. LINKING ADJECTIVES

If you want to link two or more adjectives together in Japanese, to say for example that something is delicious *and* cheap, you need to know how to make the **-te** form of the adjective.

The **-te** form is made by dropping the last **i** of the dictionary form of the adjective and adding **-kute.** Thus, the **-te** form of **samui** is **samukute.**

There are two additional bits of information you need to know about the **-te** form:
1) the **-te** form does not have a tense. It takes the tense of the last inflected expression of the sentence.

Example: *Oishikute yasui* desu.   =   It *is* good and cheap.
              Oishikute yasukatta desu.   =   It *was* good and cheap.

Therefore, the **-te** form of both **oishii** and **oishikatta** is **oishikute.**

2) The **-te** form cannot end a sentence.

As fast as you can, write the **-te** form of the following adjectives. Adjectives followed by an asterisk (*) can be found in the section on Other Adjectives.

1. takai _____

2. atsukatta _____

3. mezurashii* _____

4. oishii _____

5. chikakatta _____

6. kitanai* _____

7. suzushii _____

8. tanoshii _____

9. yokatta _____

10. furui _____

Write the **-te** form for each English adjective below.

1. hot _____

2. interesting _____

3. new _____

4. late _____

5. delicious _____

6. small _____

7. bad _____

8. far _____

9. warm _____

10. beautiful* _____

11. inexpensive _____

12. busy _____

In order to make a sentence with linked adjectives—for example, *it is cold and delicious*—you would change the first adjective to the **-te** form and add your second adjective:

It is cold   =   Tsumetai desu. (**-te** form = **tsumetakute**)
delicious   =   oishii desu

The complete sentence would be: **Tsumetakute oishii desu.**

Note that the word *and* is not expressed directly in Japanese. The concept of *and* when linking two or more adjectives is included in the **-te** form of the adjective.

Depending on the situation, the **-te** form can also show the reason for the second clause.

> Example: Furukute warui desu. =
> It is old and bad. *Or,* It is old [and so] it is bad.

Link the following sentences together using the **-te** form of the adjective. It is not necessary to repeat the subject if it is the same for both adjectives. See if you can tell whether the **-te** form simply means *and* or *and so* or either depending on context.

> Example: Sono sushi wa yasui desu.
> Sono sushi wa oishii desu.
> Ans: Sono sushi wa **yasukute oishii** desu.

1. Kore wa atarashii desu.
   Kore wa ii desu.

   _____

2. Kono koohii wa atsui desu.
   Kono koohii wa oishii desu.

   _____

3. Kono resutoran wa takakatta desu.
   Kono resutoran wa mazukatta desu.

   _____

4. Ano inu wa chiisai desu.
   Ano inu wa kawaii* desu.

   _____

5. Kono kuruma wa furui desu.
   Kono kuruma wa yoku arimasen.

   _____

6. Kono niku wa yasui desu.
   Kono niku wa atarashii desu.
   Kono niku wa oishii desu.

   _____

Use of the **-te** form does *not* necessarily mean that the last predicate of the sentence must be an adjective. The sentence may be completed with a verb, the copula (**desu** or one of its forms) or an adjective.

Example: Oishikute takusan tabemashita. = It was delicious so I ate a lot.

Translate the following sentences:

1. Sushi ga oishikute, takusan (a lot) tabemashita.

2. Kinoo wa isogashikute taihen deshita.

3. Ano inu wa ookikute takusan tabemasu.

4. Ano eiga wa omoshirokute, nido (twice) mimashita.

5. Kono kooen wa tanoshikute, mainichi kimasu.

Write these sentences in Japanese:

1. The water is cold and delicious.

2. The computer is old and so is not good.

3. That restaurant is inexpensive and good.

4. (My) eyes are red and hurt*.

5. The teacher is young and beautiful.

6. That pizza was good so I ate it everyday.

7. It's big and blue*.

8. It's unusual* and interesting.

9. The watch is small and expensive.

10. It's old and so it doesn't taste good.

    _____

11. The bus is slow and dirty*.

    _____

12. The cat is small and cute*.

    _____

12. THE -TE FORM OF NEGATIVE ADJECTIVES

What if you wanted to say, *It's not bad and it's inexpensive.* In other words, you are describing *it* as having two characteristics, *not bad* and *inexpensive*. To express this idea, you could say, **Yasukute waruku nai desu,** or you could use the negative **-te** form of **warui, waruku nakute yasui desu.**

To make the **-te** form of a negative adjective: first make the *negative plain form,* then drop the **i** from **nai** and add **-kute**.

      Example: atsui > atsuku nai > atsuku nakute

The *negative* **-te** form, like the **-te** form we have just studied, has no tense. The tense of the sentence is determined by the last inflected expression.

Try doing this exercise with the adjectives indicated:

	Neg. short form	Neg. -te form
1. ookii		
2. mazui		
3. tooi		
4. urusai*		
5. atatakai		
6. aoi*		
7. isogashii		
8. kuroi*		
9. sabishii*		
10. samui		

11. chikai _____.__

12. kawaii* _____

13. ii _____

14. yasashii _____

15. suzushii _____

As fast as you can, write the negative **-te** form of the following adjectives which are given in English:

Example: not far (and) > tooku nakute

1. not small (and) _____

2. not cheap (and) _____

3. not difficult (and) _____

4. not interesting (and) _____

5. not lonely* (and) _____

6. not cool (and) _____

7. not bad tasting (and) _____

8. not expensive (and) _____

9. not fun (and) _____

10. not unusual* (and) _____

11. not old (and) _____

12. not bad (and) _____

13. not easy (and) _____

14. not sweet (and) _____

15. not dangerous* (and) _____

The same rules apply in making a sentence with a *negative* **-te** form as for the **-te** form in the affirmative. Remember that, depending on the meaning, the **-te** form can mean either *and* or *and so.*

Try these sentences yourself:

1. The car wasn't old and so it was good.
   _____

2. The beer isn't cold so it tasted bad.
   _____

3. The meat isn't fresh so it tastes bad.
   _____

4. The dictionary isn't big so it's good.
   _____

5. Today wasn't hot so it was good.
   _____

13. Two or More Adjectives Describing a Noun

So far, we've seen cases where the **-te** form is used to link adjectives in the predicate. Let's look at cases where two or more adjectives modify a noun. If you wanted to say the phrase *a big, new house* in Japanese, you would use the **-te** form of the adjective to link it to the next. The last adjective before the noun is in the dictionary form. The phrase a *big, new house* in Japanese is: **ookikute atarashii uchi.**

Describe the following nouns with the adjectives given:

1. uchi — furui, chiisai _____

2. zasshi — yasui, omoshiroi _____

3. koora — tsumetai, oishii _____

4. hito — omoshiroi, ii _____

5. gakkoo — chikai, ii _____

6. kooen — ookii, chikai _____

7. onna no ko — chiisai, kawaii _____

8. hon — yasashii, omoshiroi _____

9. inu — ookii, kuroi _____

10. heya — kitanai, chiisai _____

By adding **desu** or one of its forms, you can make a complete sentence.

Try describing the following nouns using at least two adjectives. Make sure you write a complete sentence.

    Example: meat
              Takakute oishii niku desu.

When using more than one adjective to describe a noun, you do not mix favorable adjectives with unfavorable adjectives in the same phase. Therefore, you could not say *an expensive, ugly house.* Keep this fact in mind as you do these exercises.

1. a 280-pound weight lifter

    _____

2. a Great Dane (dog)

    _____

3. a frosty glass of ale

    _____

4. a cashmere sweater

    _____

5. a hobo

    _____

6. a car you've had for 15 years

    _____

7. Miss America

    _____

8. the super express train

    _____

Going back to the example of the *expensive, ugly house,* in Japanese, as in English, you would have to say, *It is an expensive but ugly house.* This is because you cannot mix adjectives with favorable and unfavorable connotations by using the **-te** form.

Let's take another example:
If we were to describe a soup as being both cold and delicious, we would have to say in Japanese, *It is cold but delicious soup,* since *cold* is not consistent with the idea of *delicious* when speaking of most soups. In Japanese, we would use the sentence final particle **ga** and say, Tsumetai desu **ga,** oishii suupu desu.

Translate the following sentences and see if you can understand why the idea is expressed with **ga** as opposed to the **-kute** pattern you studied previously.

1. Ookii desu ga, kitanai heya desu.

2. Furui desu ga, ii kuruma desu.

3. Atsuku nai desu ga, oishii koohii desu.

4. Kibishii desu ga, ii sensei desu.

5. Ookii desu ga, kawaii inu desu.

This last example may not be immediately clear. Although I personally think large dogs are cute partly because of their size, for the Japanese, the concept of *cute* usually implies that the object or person is small. Although the language is changing, you might still find the above way of expressing this idea clearer than **ookikute kawaii inu**.

Using the pattern: [*adj.*] **desu ga** [*adj.*] [*noun*] **desu**, describe the following nouns with the adjectives indicated:

1. coffee (cold yet delicious)

2. park (small but good)

3. cat (small but scary)

4. book (difficult but interesting)

5. magazine (expensive but interesting)

6. post office (large but not good)

7. shoes (expensive, but good)

8. beer (cheap, but delicious)

9. sushi (not good but cheap)

_____

10. explanation (detailed but difficult)

_____

In the following exercise, decide whether to use the **-kute** form for compatible adjectives or the **ga** pattern above for adjectives which are conflicting in connotation. Write complete Japanese sentences.

Example: Oishikute yasui sushi desu. = It's inexpensive and good sushi.
Oishiku nai desu ga, takai sushi desu. = It's sushi that's expensive but not good.

1. coffee (hot, delicious)

_____

2. dog (large, cute)

_____

3. house (big, old)

_____

4. park (big, dirty)

_____

5. school (nearby, good)

_____

6. teacher (strict, good)

_____

7. magazine (not interesting, expensive)

_____

8. clock (old, good)

_____

9. sweater (warm, inexpensive)

_____

10. sushi (delicious, cheap)

_____

14. PERMISSION

The **-kute** form is also used to ask as well as to give permission. You can use this form to ask such questions as *Is it OK if it's inexpensive?* or to say *It's fine if it's not new.*

The pattern for this construction is:

Question : **-te** form **mo ii desu ka?**

Statement: **-te** form **mo ii desu.**

This pattern can be used for both negative and affirmative **-te** forms.

Example: Yasukute mo ii desu.　　= It's OK if it's cheap.
Yasuku nakute mo ii desu.　= It's OK if it's not cheap.

Sometimes in conversation, the **mo** is dropped so that you hear **yasukute ii desu.**

What permission is being asked here?

1. Koohii wa tsumetakute mo ii desu ka?

2. Hon wa omoshiroku nakute mo ii desu ka?

3. Mondai wa muzukashikute mo ii desu ka?

4. Tenki wa yoku nakute mo ii desu ka?

Try asking permission for the following. Refer to the sentences above if you have difficulty. Use the full pattern including **mo.**

1. Is it OK if it's easy ?

2. Is it OK if the beer is not cold?

3. Is it OK if the computer is not new?

   _____

4. Is it OK if the paper is white?

   _____

5. Is it OK if the school is faraway?

   _____

6. Is it OK if the explanation is not detailed?

   _____

7. Is it OK if the pen is red?

   _____

8. Is it OK if it isn't warm?

   _____

9. Is it OK if it is dirty?

   _____

10. Is it OK if it is slow?

    _____

Now, give permission by omitting the question particle **ka.**

1. It's OK if it's small.

   _____

2. It's fine if the coffee is cold.

   _____

3. It doesn't matter if the newspaper is old.

   _____

4. It's all right if the tickets are expensive.

   _____

5. It doesn't matter if the pen is not black.

   _____

6. It's OK if the vegetables are not fresh.

   _____

7. It doesn't matter if the house is dirty.

   _____

8. It doesn't matter if the cat isn't cute.

   _____

9. It's OK if the weather is bad.

   _____

10. It's OK if the curry isn't spicy.

    _____

The pattern you have just studied, **-kute mo ii desu,** is the formal form. If you were speaking with a friend or a person younger and/or inferior in rank to yourself, you could use the plain form, **-kute mo ii.** If you were asking permission, a man could say, **-kute mo ii kai?** but a woman would have to say, **-kute mo ii no?** It is sometimes tricky for a foreign speaker to know when to use a friendlier form of speech. When in doubt, always opt for the more polite forms.

At the other end of the spectrum is the super polite form, **-kute mo kamaimasen ka?** and **-kute mo kamaimasen.** This form has the same meaning as **-kute mo ii desu** although it looks different because of the negative **-masen** ending.

Thus:

Yasukute mo ii desu. = Yasukute mo kamaimasen.
(It's OK if it's inexpensive).

Change these sentences to the plain, formal, or super-polite form as indicated in parentheses.

1. Takakute mo ii desu. (plain, man)

2. Atsukute mo ii ka? (super-polite)

3. Tsumetaku nakute mo ii desu ka? (plain, woman)

4. Samukute ii. (formal)

5. Furukute mo kamaimasen ka? (formal)

6. Atarashiku nakute mo ii desu. (plain, man)

7. Omoshiroku nakute ii no? (formal)

8. Yoku nakute mo ii. (super-polite)

9. Akakute mo ii desu ka? (super-polite)

10. Chikaku nakute mo ii. (formal)

15. -KUTE WA IKEMASEN

Suppose someone asked you **Yasukute mo ii desu ka?** and your answer was no. It is possible to express this with the **-kute** form also.

The pattern is:
    -kute wa ikemasen or **-kute wa dame desu**

    Example: Yasukute mo ii desu ka?   =   Is it OK if it's cheap?

                Iie. Yasukute wa ikemasen. =   No. It's no good if it's cheap.

    OR

                Iie. Yasukute wa dame desu.

A word of caution: the **-kute wa ikemasen** and **-kute wa dame desu** are strong prohibitions. Generally, they are accompanied by some sort of explanation, such as "The inexpensive one doesn't come with a warranty so **yasukute wa ikemasen**."

Using the above pattern, answer *No, it's not OK if . . .*

1. Kuruma wa furukute mo ii desu ka?
    _____

2. Mondai wa yasashikute mo ii desu ka?
    _____

3. Pen wa kurokute mo kamaimasen ka?
    _____

4. Hana wa akakute mo ii desu ka?
    _____

5. Kippu wa yasukute mo ii desu ka?
    _____

6. Kutsu wa ookikute mo kamaimasen ka?
    _____

The **-kute wa ikemasen ka?** may be considered an alternate (and commonly used) way of asking permission. Its politeness level is comparable to **-te mo kamaimasen ka?**

By the same token, **-kute wa dame desu ka?** can be used to ask permission. Its politeness level roughly approximates that of **-te mo ii desu ka?**

Keep in mind that with **ikemasen** and **dame desu** in this pattern, the particle used is **wa**.

Now, you have a variety of ways at your disposal to ask permission using adjectives.

Example: Is it OK if it's hot?

Super polite: Atsukute mo kamaimasen ka?
Super polite: Atsukute wa ikemasen ka?
Formal: Atsukute mo ii desu ka?
Formal: Atsukute wa dame desu ka?
Friendly: Atsukute mo ii? (man) / Atsukute mo ii no? (woman)

Try these examples yourself:

1. Is it all right if it's expensive?
   Super polite: _____
   Super polite: _____
   Formal: _____
   Friendly: _____

2. Is it OK if the beer is not cold?
   Super polite: _____
   Super polite: _____
   Friendly (man): _____
   Friendly (woman): _____

3. Is it OK if it is not new?
   Super polite: _____
   Formal: _____
   Formal: _____
   Friendly (woman): _____

4. Is it OK if the curry is spicy?
   Super polite: _____
   Super polite: _____
   Formal: _____
   Formal: _____

5. Is it OK if it's not white?

   Super polite: _____

   Formal: _____

   Friendly (man): _____

   Friendly (woman): _____

16. THE -BA FORM

The **-ba** form is the *if* or conditional form. It is used in cases where a condition is placed on an action or thing. It is sometimes translated as *provided that, as long as,* or just *if.* Examples of English sentences having a conditional clause are: *If it's red,* I'll buy it, and, I'll watch it *provided it is interesting.*

In Japanese, the words *if* and *provided that* are not expressed. Instead, this concept is incorporated in the **-ba** form of the adjective.

The **-ba** form of any adjective is created by dropping the last **i** and adding **-kereba.**

> Example: atsui > atsu > atsukereba

The **-ba** form of **ii** is **yokereba**, from **yoi.**

The clause **atsukereba** means *if it's hot, provided it's hot,* etc. It is a clause and not a full sentence and must be followed by another clause.

> Example: atsukereba ii desu. = If it's hot, it is good.

Give the **-ba** forms for the following adjectives:

1. samui _____

2. chiisai _____

3. tsuyoi* _____

4. urusai* _____

5. ii _____

6. tanoshii _____

7. hayai _____

8. atatakai _____

9. mazushii* _____

10. aoi* _____

11. isogashii _____

12. kuwashii* _____

13. muzukashii _____

14. chikai _____

15. warui _____

16. osoi _____

17. yasashii _____

18. kitanai* _____

19. ookii _____

20. furui _____

Now, give a Japanese equivalent for these phrases:

1. If it is far _____

2. Provided it is small _____

3. As long as it's good _____

4. If it is near _____

5. Provided it is cheap _____

6. As long as it's easy _____

7. If you are busy _____

8. If it is cool _____

9. If you are lonely _____

10. As long as it's fun _____

11. Provided it's new _____

12. If it's early _____

13. Provided it's slow _____

14. As long as it's tasty _____

15. Provided you're happy _____

Let's combine some of these *if clauses* with **ii desu** to make a complete sentence.

> Example: Juusu ga tsumetakereba, ii desu. = As long as the juice is cold, it's fine.

Notice that the subject of **tsumetakereba** is **juusu** and it is marked with the particle **ga**. Usually, the subject of **-ba** clauses is marked with **ga.**

In English, the *if* clause may appear at the beginning or end of the sentence. However, in Japanese, it must *always* appear at the beginning, as the **-ba** clause cannot end a sentence. Therefore, the **-ba** form is neither formal nor informal. It has no level, thus it can be used with all levels of speech.

1. If it's near, it's good.

   _____

2. It's fine if the coffee is hot.

   _____

3. It's fine as long as the weather is good.

   _____

4. If it's inexpensive, it's fine.

   _____

5. It's fine as long as it's small.

   _____

6. It's OK as long as it's warm.

   _____

7. It's fine provided it's near.

   _____

8. If they're white, it's fine.

   _____

9. It's OK as long as it's fun.

   _____

10. It's fine if you're happy.

    _____

If you are going to use a verb in the second part of the sentence, it *must* be in a non-non-past tense.

Here are some verbs:

ikimasu	(I, you, he, etc.)	will go
yomimasu	"	will read
nomimasu	"	will drink
kaimasu	"	will buy
tabemasu	"	will eat
kikimasu	"	will listen
mimasu	"	will see, watch
deeto shimasu	"	will go on a date
tetsudaimasu	"	will help, assist
sooji shimasu	"	will clean

Choose a verb to end the following **-ba** clauses in a meaningful manner. Write your intended meaning on the second line.

1. Sushi ga oishikereba, _____
   Eng. _____

2. Sono zasshi ga yasukereba, _____

   _____

3. Heya ga kitanakereba, _____

   _____

4. Anata ga isogashikereba, _____

_____

5. Sono hon ga yasashikereba, _____

_____

6. Tenki ga yokereba, _____

_____

7. Sono hito ga yasashikereba, _____

_____

8. Sono ongaku ga yokereba, _____

_____

9. Koohii ga atsukereba, _____

_____

10. Sono terebi bangumi ga omoshirokereba, _____

_____

Answer the following questions using a conditional clause:

1. Ashita ikimasu ka?

_____

2. Ongaku o kikimasu ka?

_____

3. Nihon no shinbun o yomimasu ka?

_____

4. Sono seetaa o kaimasu ka?

_____

5. Tempura o tabemasu ka?

_____

6. Sono hito to deeto o shimasu ka?

_____

7. Sono heya o sooji shimasu ka?

_____

8. Watashi o tetsudaimasu ka?

_____

9. Sono eiga o mimasu ka?

   _____

10. Juusu o nomimasu ka?

    _____

An application of the **-ba** form is used in such expressions as _the hotter the better._ Note the placement of the **-ba** form and the _dictionary_ form:

Koohii wa _atsukereba atsui hodo ii_ desu. = As far as coffee is concerned, _the hotter the better._

Although **ii desu** is used when you want to say _the [adj.] the better,_ other adjectives may be used to end the sentence.

For example:
Ookikereba ookii hodo takai desu. = The larger it is, the more expensive.

What do the following sentences mean?

1. Mondai wa muzukashikereba muzukashii hodo omoshiroi desu.

   _____

2. Daiya wa ookikereba ookii hodo takai desu.

   _____

3. Baiorin (violin) wa furukereba furui hodo takai desu.

   _____

4. Suupu wa atsukereba atsui hodo oishii desu.

   _____

5. Biiru wa tsumetakereba tsumetai hodo oishii desu.

   _____

6. Yasai wa atarashikereba atarashii hodo oishii desu.

   _____

Now apply the **-kereba** [_adj._] **hodo** form for the following adjectives:

Example: hot
           atsukereba atsui hodo

1. difficult

   _____

2. small

   _____

3. expensive

   _____

4. delicious

   _____

5. strict*

   _____

6. busy

   _____

7. large

   _____

8. new/fresh

   _____

9. interesting

   _____

10. easy

    _____

11. spicy

    _____

12. sweet

    _____

Now, place some of the above expressions into full sentences. Don't be fooled by the English wording. In Japanese, they all follow the pattern illustrated in the above two exercises.

1. The faster it is, the better.

   _____

2. As for curry rice, the spicier it is, the more delicious it is.

   _____

3. As for soup, the hotter it is, the better it is.

   _____

4. As far as teachers are concerned, the stricter they are, the better they are.

   _____

5. As for cars, the newer (they are) the better (they are).

   _____

6. As far as tests go, the easier the better.

   _____

7. As for diamonds, the bigger the better.

   _____

8. As for computers, the newer they are, the more expensive they are.

   _____

9. As far as cars go, the older they are, the cheaper they are.

   _____

10. As far as work goes, the busier I am, the better.

    _____

11. As far as movies go, the older they are, the more interesting they are.

    _____

12. As far as explanations go, the more detailed they are, the better.

    _____

17. THE NEGATIVE -BA FORM

The negative **-ba** form is used to express the idea *if it is not . . . , provided it is not . . . , as long as it is not . . .*

It is formed by dropping the last **i** from the dictionary form of the adjective and adding **-ku nakereba** as in **atsuku nakereba,** "if it's *not* hot."

Example: atsui > atsu > atsuku nakereba

Give the negative **-ba** form for the following adjectives. Do the exercise without stopping, as fast as you can.

1. mazui _____

2. tsumetai _____

3. osoi _____

4. tooi _____

5. tanoshii _____

6. ookii _____

7. oishii _____

8. ii _____

9. urusai* _____

10. tsuyoi* _____

11. ureshii* _____

12. chiisai _____

13. atarashii _____

14. yasui _____

15. muzukashii _____

16. kuroi* _____

17. furui _____

18. takai _____

19. kawaii* _____

20. kowai* _____

Use the English cues and write the negative **-ba** form for the following:

1. If it's not close _____

2. If it's not red* _____

3. If it's not new _____

4. If it's not scary* _____

5. If you're not busy _____

6. If it's not easy _____

7. If it's not far _____

8. If it's not dirty* _____

9. If it's not beautiful* _____

10. If it's not warm _____

For the next set of exercises, let's add the verb **irimasen** meaning *I don't want it* or *I don't need it.*

Mixed drill. Express these sentences in Japanese. Read the English carefully: some require the affirmative **-ba** form, while others require the negative.

Example: Tsumetaku nakereba, irimasen = If it's not cold, I don't want it.

1. If it's *not* hot, I don't want it.

_____

2. If it's small, I don't want it.

_____

3. If it's *not* difficult, I don't want it.

_____

4. If it's easy, I don't need it.

_____

5. If it's *not* warm, I don't need it.

_____

6. If it's dirty, I don't want it.

_____

7. If it *doesn't* taste good, I don't want it.

_____

8. If it's expensive, I don't want it.

_____

Answer the following questions using a *negative* **-ba** form as a condition.

Example: Q: Koohii o nomimasu ka? = Will you drink the coffee?
            A: Tsumetaku nakereba nomimasu. = If it's not cold, I'll drink it.

1. Kyoo ikimasu ka?

_____

2. Kyoo benkyoo shimasu ka?

_____

3. Sono kutsu o kaimasu ka?

_____

4. Sono shinbun o yomimasu ka?

_____

One common use for the **-ku nakereba** form is the construction **-ku nakereba narimasen** meaning *it must be, it has to be.* The addition of **narimasen** to the *negative* **-ba** form makes it a complete sentence. The **-masen** form is a formal or polite level of speech.

Example: Akaku nakereba narimasen. = It has to be red.

Try the following sentences. Be careful to write all the syllables correctly. Sound out each syllable as you write!

1. It has to be black.* _____

2. It has to be near. _____

3. It has to be hot. _____

4. It has to be interesting. _____

5. It has to be blue.* _____

6. It has to be good. _____

7. I have to be busy. _____

8. It has to be new. _____

9. It has to be inexpensive. _____

10. It has to be fast. _____

11. It has to be small. _____

12. He has to be strong.* _____

When you add a subject, such as *beer, sweater, newspaper,* etc., that subject can be marked by the particle **wa** or the particle **ga.**

Example: Biiru wa tsumetaku nakereba narimasen. = Beer must be cold.

1. The teacher must be strict.*

_____

2. The weather must be good.

_____

3. The team has to be strong.

_____

4. The magazines have to be interesting.

_____

18. -SOO NOT SOO

In order to express the idea that something looks or appears to be red, happy, etc., you must convert the adjective to its **-soo** form. This is a distinct form from the **soo** form studied earlier, both in terms of its meaning and morphology (how it is formed from the adjective).

You change an adjective to its **-soo** form by dropping the last **i** of the adjective in its dictionary form and adding **-soo.**

Example: atsui > atsu > atsusoo = looks, appears hot.

The only exception to this rule is the adjective **ii**. The **-soo** form of **ii** is **yosasoo**.

Write the **-soo** form of the following adjectives:

1. oishii _____

2. mazui _____

3. chiisai _____

4. kibishii* _____

5. itai* _____

6. takai _____

7. ii _____

8. tsuyoi* _____

9. furui _____

10. omoshiroi _____

11. samui _____

12. suzushii_____

13. ureshii*_____

14. sabishii*_____

15. yasashii_____

The **-soo** form does not end a sentence. One way to end the sentence would be to add **desu** or one of its forms.

The **-soo** form is used to make a statement about a person, thing, or situation based on *visual* evaluation. If you see a strawberry shortcake with mounds of fresh strawberries and cream, you could say **"Oishisoo desu"** before tasting it, because, based on your observation, the cake appears to be delicious. This form is also used to comment on the states of others, as the Japanese would not presume to speak with certainty about the emotions or feelings of others.

Example: Atsusoo deshita.   =   He looked hot.
            Atsusoo ja arimasen.   =   He doesn't look hot.

Try this exercise using the **-soo** form and **desu**. Remember, it is not necessary to translate subject pronouns such as *I, she,* etc.

1. She looks cold.
    _____

2. He looks lonely*.
    _____

3. It looks painful*.
    _____

4. They look happy*.
    _____

5. She looks strict*.
    _____

6. He looks strong*.
    _____

7. It looks delicious.
    _____

8. It looks old.
    _____

9. You look busy.

_____

10. It looks good.

_____

Next, use the **-soo** form to describe the following situations. Be sure to make a complete sentence by adding the word **desu** at the end.

1. You see a frosty glass of soda. How does it appear?

    _____

2. You see a man with bulging biceps. How does he appear?

    _____

3. You see a group of kids coming home from the last day of school before summer vacation. How do they look?

    _____

4. You meet your friend who has just been dumped by his girlfriend. How does he look?

    _____

5. Your math prof hands you an equation with 4 variables to solve for. How does it look?

    _____

6. The meat in the package at the supermarket is green and brown. How does it look?

    _____

7. Your Japanese teacher is a thin woman with her hair in a tight bun. Her lips are always pursed. How does she appear?

    _____

When an adjective in the **-soo** form modifies a noun, the particle **na** must be used after it.

Example: sabishisoo na hito = a lonely-looking person, a person who looks lonely

Some nouns you have come across:

hito	=	person, people
kodomo	=	child, children
otoko no hito	=	man, men

onna no hito	=	woman, women
ryoori	=	food, cuisine
michi	=	road, street

See if you can write the following phrases using the **-soo** form:

1. delicious-looking food

    _____

2. a man who looks strong

    _____

3. a teacher who looks strict

    _____

4. a warm-looking sweater

    _____

5. water which looks cold

    _____

6. a dangerous-looking street

    _____

7. a sweet-looking woman

    _____

8. a happy-looking child

    _____

9. a seemingly difficult problem

    _____

10. an expensive-looking dress

    _____

11. a person who looks lonely

    _____

19. I Think That . . .

Another setting for adjectives is the pattern **to omoimasu**, *I think that* . . .

As in the pattern **soo desu**, the plain form of the adjective is placed before **to omoimasu.**

> Example: Yokatta to omoimasu. = I think it was good.

Whereas in English, the phrase *I think that* appears at the beginning of the sentence, in Japanese, **to omoimasu** always appears at the end.

In Japanese, the subject of **omoimasu** is usually *I,* as one would not presume to state with certainty what someone else thinks. In addition, the adjective can have its own subject which is marked by the particles **wa** or **ga.**

> Example: Eiga wa omoshirokatta to omoimasu. = I think the movie was interesting.

The level of the above example is polite even though the preceding adjective is in the plain form.

Let's practice this pattern with **omoimasu.** What is being said here?

1. Sasaki-san wa isogashii to omoimasu.

    _____

2. Sono sushi wa mazukatta to omoimasu.

    _____

3. Ano yuubinkyoku wa anmari tooku nai to omoimasu.

    _____

4. Kinoo wa totemo samukatta to omoimasu.

    _____

5. Kono yasai wa oishiku nai to omoimasu.

    _____

Try these yourself in Japanese. Pay attention to the tense of the adjective. You may use either **wa** or **ga** after the subject of the adjective, in these cases.

1. I think that it's hot.

   _____

2. I think that it was good.

   _____

3. I think that it's not far.

   _____

4. I think that the house was near.

   _____

5. I think that the tickets were not very expensive.

   _____

6. I think that he's not busy today.

   _____

7. I think that the house is quite small.

   _____

8. I think that the weather is usually warm.

   _____

9. I think that the weather wasn't bad.

   _____

10. I think that the school was big.

    _____

11. I think that buses aren't fast.

    _____

12. I think that the meat wasn't fresh.

    _____

13. I think that it's not late.

    _____

14. I think that the test was easy.

    _____

15. I think that the car was quite new.

    _____

20. Hoshii!

The adjective **hoshii** is equivalent to the verb formation *I want,* when it is used with a *noun.*

> Example: Pan ga hoshii desu. = I want bread.

Bear these two rules in mind regarding **hoshii**:

1) **hoshii** can be inflected in all tenses (past, non-past, etc.) like any other adjective in Japanese.

2) As **hoshii** is *not* a verb, you can *never* use the particle **o** for the thing you want. *Usually,* in the affirmative, the thing you want will be marked by the particle **ga** (as opposed to **wa**). *Usually,* in the negative, the thing you don't or didn't want will be marked by **wa** (as opposed to **ga**).

In a statement, the person who wants is the speaker, so we translate it into English using the pronoun *I.*

> Example: Pan ga hoshii. = I want bread.

The above sentence can never mean, *She wants bread,* as the Japanese do not speak with certainty about what another person wants. The addition of such expressions as **soo desu** or **deshoo**, however, will allow you to do so.

Of course, **hoshii** can be used in question form as in:

> Nani ga hoshii desu ka? = What do you want?

Try these inflections of **hoshii**: (Do not translate the word *it*).

I want it. (formal) _____

I want it. (plain) _____

I don't want it. (formal) _____

I don't want it. (plain) _____

I wanted it. (formal) _____

I wanted it. (plain) _____

I didn't want it. (formal) _____

I didn't want it. (plain) _____

Keeping in mind the rule for particle use from the previous page, write these sentences in Japanese. Use either formal or plain forms.

1. I wanted [some] bread.

   _____

2. I don't want a new car.

   _____

3. I wanted a color TV.

   _____

4. I didn't want a newspaper.

   _____

5. I wanted fresh veggies.

   _____

6. I don't want a detailed explanation.

   _____

7. I didn't want the sushi.

   _____

8. What do you want?

   _____

9. I wanted the red shoes.

   _____

10. I don't want the black shirts.

    _____

11. I don't want them at all.

    _____

12. I don't want it very much.

    _____

13. I didn't want coffee.

    _____

14. Did you want tempura?

    _____

15. I don't want a new computer.

    _____

21. COLOR WORDS

All adjectives denoting colors in Japanese have a corresponding noun form as well. There is no difference in meaning between the noun and adjective forms for these colors. Thus, **akai** means *red* and the corresponding noun form, **aka** also means *red*.

Here is a list of adjectives denoting color and their corresponding noun forms:

Adjective	Noun	Meaning
akai	aka	red
aoi	ao	blue or green
shiroi	shiro	white
kuroi	kuro	black
kiiroi	kiiro	yellow

When you modify or describe a noun with an adjective, all you have to do is place the adjective in front of the noun. You do *not* need a particle between the adjective and noun. You have already seen this with your work with adjectives so far. If, however, you modify a noun with another noun, you need to insert the particle **no** between them.

Example: kiiroi hana = yellow flower

BUT

kiiro *no* hana = yellow flower

The above two expressions are equivalent in meaning. One is simply a variation of the other.

In this exercise, change the part of speech of the word denoting color and add or omit the particle **no** as needed.

1. kuroi kaban > _____

2. kiiroi doresu > _____

3. ao no shatsu > _____

4. shiroi kami > _____

5. aka no seetaa > _____

There are certain exceptions to this pattern, that is, [*color*] + **no** + [*noun*]. Notice that the particle **no** is dropped in the following:

aozora   = blue sky
ao shingoo   = green light
aka shingoo = red light
guriinsha   = a first class car (of a train)
guriinken   = a first class ticket
kurokami   = black hair

Names of certain colors exist only in *noun* form. Among these are names for colors which have been borrowed from English, as well as native Japanese terms.

Examples of these are:

Noun	*Meaning*
chairo	brown
midori-iro	green (the green that exists in nature)
pinku	pink
nebii buruu	navy blue
guree	gray
guriin	green
beeju	beige
rabendaa	lavender

Since the above words are nouns, they must be followed by the particle **no** when describing a noun.

Translate the following phrases. Look up any nouns you don't know in the glossary.

1. a brown bag _____

2. red light _____

3. pink flowers _____

4. a navy blue suit _____

5. a gray skirt _____

6. a lavendar sweater _____

7. green light _____

8. a beige dress _____

9. blue sky _____

10. a first-class ticket _____

You *must* use the noun form of a color word when you describe something with more than one color. The particle **to** is used to mean *and* when it connects two nouns.

Example: It was *white and black.*   = *Shiro* **to** *kuro* deshita.
           It was a *white and black* sweater. = *Shiro* **to** *kuro* no seetaa deshita.

In the second example above, the noun **seetaa** is being described by the color nouns, **shiro** and **kuro**, hence, the use of the particle **no**.

Now, translate the following phrases using the particle **to**.

1. a black and beige sweater

    _____

2. lavender and red socks

    _____

3. a brown and white dog

_____

4. a blue and pink suit

_____

5. a red and yellow tie

_____

6. a black and beige skirt

_____

7. a red and black bag

_____

8. a yellow and pink shirt

_____

You *must* use the *noun* form of the color if it is the subject or object of the predicate. For example, in the sentence, *Red is good, Red* is the subject of the sentence. In Japanese, you *must* use the word **aka** because an adjective in its dictionary form cannot be used as the subject of a sentence.

Example: Aka ga ii desu. = Red is good (fine, OK).

Suki desu means *I like [it]*. To say that you like a color, use the particle **ga** after the name of the color you like.

Example: Aka ga suki desu. = I like red. (Red is likeable to me.)

In the example above, **aka** is the subject of **suki desu**.

Use one of the appropriate sentence patterns above to do this next exercise:

1. I like yellow. _____

2. Brown is good. _____

3. I like pink. _____

4. Blue is good. _____

5. Do you like lavender? _____

6. Is black OK? _____

7. Do you like gray and brown? _____

8. Blue and white are fine. _____

9. I like red, white and blue. _____

10. Are green and white good? _____

22. ANOTHER PATTERN WITH COLORS

In English, we often attach the ending *-ish* to the names of colors as in *whitish, pinkish, yellowish*. We can do a similar operation in Japanese to arrive at words with similar meanings.

In Japanese, you use the *noun* form of the color and add the ending **-ppoi.**

> Example: shiro (white) > shiroppoi (whitish)

The resulting word, **shiroppoi,** means *whitish, of whitish hue,* or *white looking.*

Note that **shiroppoi** is an *adjective,* although the word we started with was a noun. As an adjective, **shiroppoi** can modify a noun as in **shiroppoi suutsu,** or it can be used in the predicate, as in **shiroppoi desu.**

Further, **shiroppoi** can be inflected in the same way as any other adjective.

Try these inflections:

1. Is it whitish? _____

2. It's not whitish. (formal) _____

3. It was whitish. (plain) _____

4. It wasn't whitish. (formal) _____

5. It's not whitish. (plain) _____

6. It became whitish. _____

Give the **-ppoi** form for the following:

1. reddish _____

2. whitish _____

3. yellowish _____

4. bluish _____

5. blackish _____

What do these phrases mean?

1. kuroppoi inu _____

2. akappoi seetaa _____

3. aoppoi sukaato _____

4. chairoppoi kaban _____

5. shiroppoi biru _____

6. kiiroppoi sora _____

7. akappoi kao _____

Next, try to incorporate some of these **-ppoi** phrases into sentences. You can either modify a noun with **-ppoi** or you can place the **-ppoi** adjective in the predicate. In the latter case, be sure to inflect it to the proper form.

1. I saw a dog [with] a black [coat].

   _____

2. The sky was yellowish.

   _____

3. It turned (became) brownish.

   _____

4. I bought a reddish sweater.

   _____

5. It's sort of a white-colored building.

   _____

23. THE -SA FORM

An adjective can be made into a *noun* by dropping the last **-i** of the adjective and adding **-sa**.

Example: atsui > atsu > atsusa

The resulting *noun* **atsusa** means *heat,* and it is used to mean the degree or type of heat as in *I can't stand this [type, degree]* heat, or *The* heat *[type] of the desert differs from that of the tropics.* Another way to think of **atsusa** is *heat* as in *hotness.* **Atsusa** cannot be used in sentences such as *I don't like the* heat, or *In the* heat *of the moment, she said some pretty horrible things.*

Here are more examples of adjectives in the **-sa** form:

-sa *form*	*Meaning*
ookisa	size ("largeness," how big)
tsuyosa	strength (how strong)
hayasa	speed (how fast)
yosa	how good

In this exercise, write the **-sa** form next to the adjective and give its meaning on the line below. Sometimes there will not be a one-word translation for the **-sa** form. If you get stuck, think of "degree of," "type of."

1. muzukashii >
    _____

2. ookii >
    _____

3. mezurashii* >
    _____

4. oishii >
    _____

5. atarashii >
    _____

6. kibishii >

_____

7. wakai* >

_____

8. sabishii* >

_____

9. itai* >

_____

10. mazushii* >

_____

We can make a complete sentence using the above **-sa** form in the following pattern:

Sore wa _atsusa **ni yorimasu**_. = That depends on _how hot_ it is.
That depends on the _degree_ to which it is hot.

Sore wa **sensei no kibishisa** ni yorimasu. = That depends on _how strict_ the teacher is.

In the following exercise, change the _italicized_ words to the **-sa** form of the appropriate adjective and translate into Japanese as in the above example:

1. That depends on _how busy_ I am.

_____

2. That depends on _how hard_ the problem is.

_____

3. That depends on _how large_ the house is.

_____

4. That depends on _how cold_ it is.

_____

5. That depends on _how new_ the car is.

_____

6. That depends on _how interesting_ the book is.

_____

7. That depends on _how fast_ the train is.

_____

8. That depends on _how sweet_ the candy is.

_____

9. That depends on _how detailed_ the explanation is.

_____

10. That depends on *how good* the TV is.

_____

Answer these questions using the **-sa** form and the **ni yorimasu** pattern:

1. Nihon no uchi wa takai desu ka?

    _____

2. Mainichi tenisu ni ikimasu ka?

    _____

3. Okashi o tabemasu ka?

    _____

4. Karee raisu ga suki desu ka?

    _____

5. Nihongo no hon o yomimasu ka?

    _____

Another pattern that will help you learn the meaning of the **-sa** form is:

____-sa ni bikkuri shimashita. = I was surprised at how _____ it was.

Example: Chuusha no itasa ni bikkuri shimashita. =
           I was surprised at *how painful* the injection was.

Using the **-sa** form and the **ni bikkuri** pattern, try these sentences:

1. I was surprised at *how cold* it was.

    _____

2. I was surprised at *how hot* Japan was.

    _____

3. I was surprised at *how difficult* the test was.

    _____

4. I was surprised at *how strong* the team was.

    _____

5. I was surprised at *how big* the house was.

    _____

6. I was surprised at *how old* the TV was.

    _____

7. I was surprised at *how cheap* the tickets were.

   _____

8. I was surprised at *how fast* the Shinkansen was.

   _____

9. I was surprised at *how hot* it was.

   _____

10. I was surprised at *how cold* the water was.

    _____

24. THE -TARI -TARI FORM

The **-tari -tari** form of adjectives is used to indicate intermittent or alternating contrasting states.

> Example: Sometimes it's difficult and sometimes it's easy.

This form is made by adding **ri** to the *past tense* of the adjective and then adding some form of **desu** or **shimasu**.

> Example: Samukattari atsukattari shimasu. = Sometimes it's cold and sometimes it's hot.
>
> Takakattari yasukattari desu. = Sometimes they're expensive and sometimes they're cheap.
>
> Tsumetakattari shimasu. = Sometimes it's cold.

Although the formal non-past forms of **shimasu** and **desu** are used in the examples above, any form (including plain and past) of these can be used to end the sentence. If, for instance, you want to say *Sometimes it was hot and sometimes it was cold,* all you would do is change the ending **shimasu** in the first example to **shimashita**. However, negative forms of **shimasu** and **desu** are never used with **-tari -tari**.

Of **shimasu** and **desu**, **shimasu** seems to be the choice of most Japanese speakers.

Give the **-tari -tari shimasu** form of the following adjectives and write the meaning in English below.

1. atsui/samui _____
   (Eng.) _____

2. ookii/chiisai _____
   _____

3. tooi/chikai _____
   _____

4. atarashii/furui _____

_____

5. kuroi/shiroi _____

_____

6. ii/warui _____

_____

7. takai/yasui _____

_____

8. amai/karai _____

_____

What do these sentences mean?

1. Nihon no uchi wa chiisakattari ookikattari shimasu.

_____

2. Sensei wa yasashikattari kibishikattari shimashita.

_____

3. Sono resutoran no tempura wa oishikattari mazukattari desu.

_____

4. Fuyu wa samukattari attakattari shimasu.

_____

5. Sono densha wa hayakattari osokattari shimasu.

_____

Express these sentences in Japanese:

1. Sometimes it's expensive and sometimes it's cheap.

_____

2. Sometimes they're large and sometimes they're small.

_____

3. Sometimes it's near and sometimes it's far.

_____

4. Summers are sometimes cool and sometimes hot.

5. The buses are sometimes early and sometimes late.

6. The vegetables are sometimes fresh and sometimes old.

7. I sometimes feel lonely.

8. The coffee is sometimes good and sometimes bad (tasting).

9. The curry rice is spicy at times and sweet at other times.

10. The Japanese teachers were sometimes strict and sometimes sweet.

11. The tests are sometimes difficult and sometimes easy.

12. The weather is sometimes good and sometimes bad.

The **-tari -tari** form is also a convenient way of expressing such ideas as *Sometimes it's hot and sometimes it's not*. The formula for this construction is [past form of the adj.] **ri** [negative plain past form of the adj.] **ri shimasu**.

Example: Yokattari yokunakattari shimasu. = Sometimes it's good and sometimes it's not.

Express the following sentences in Japanese:

1. Sometimes it's hot and sometimes it's not.

2. Sometimes I'm busy and sometimes I'm not.

3. Sometimes it's fun and sometimes it's not.

4. Sometimes they were expensive and sometimes not.

5. Sometimes the bus is fast and sometimes not.

6. Sometimes the tests are difficult and sometimes not.

7. Sometimes the dogs are large and sometimes not.

   _____

8. Sometimes the bread is fresh and sometimes not.

   _____

9. Sometimes the food is good and sometimes not.

   _____

10. Sometimes the books are interesting and sometimes not.

    _____

11. Sometimes the tests are easy and sometimes not.

    _____

12. Sometimes the textbooks are inexpensive and sometimes not.

    _____

Answer the following questions using the **-tari -tari** form or the _negative_ **-tari -tari** form.

1. Nihon no shinbun wa muzukashii desu ka?

   _____

2. Amerika no uchi wa ookii desu ka?

   _____

3. Ano mise no sushi wa doo desu ka?

   _____

4. Nihon no kuruma wa yasui desu ka?

   _____

5. Nihongo no sensei wa doo desu ka?

   _____

6. Mondai wa yasashii desu ka?

   _____

7. Furansu no eiga wa omoshiroi desu ka?

   _____

8. Densha wa hayai desu ka?

   _____

25. SUGIMASU — "IT'S TOO . . ."

An interesting construction using adjectives involves the use of the adjective stem added to the verb -**sugimasu** to mean that something is too or excessively *red, difficult,* etc.

The adjective stem is the adjective minus -**i**.

    Example: atsui > atsu
                    samui > samu

To say that something is *too hot,* you would simply add -**sugimasu** to **atsu** to form **atsusugimasu**. The subject of the predicate is marked by either the particle **wa** or **ga**.

    Example: Kono koohii wa atsusugimasu. = This coffee is too hot.

Sugimasu is a verb in its formal non-past form. The past tense of **sugimasu** is **sugimashita**.

Do the following exercise using **sugimasu** or **sugimashita**.

1. It's too cold.

    _____

2. It was too hot.

    _____

3. She's too strict.*

    _____

4. It was too noisy.

    _____

5. It's too old.

    _____

6. The dress is too cheap.

    _____

7. The problem is too difficult.

    _____

8. Winters are too cold.

    _____

9. The curry rice is too spicy.

_____

10. The cake was too sweet.

_____

11. The dictionary is too old.

_____

12. The teacher is too young.*

_____

13. The house was too small.

_____

14. This coffee is too awful.

_____

15. The Coke is too cold.

_____

The following questions will ask you how something is, using **doo desu ka?**
Answer using the **-sugimasu** form.

> Example: Kono koohii wa doo desu ka? = How is the coffee?
>   Chotto atsusugimasu ne. = It's a little too hot.

Chotto softens the statement and translates well into English as _little, slightly, a bit._
The sentence final particle **ne** is used to invite the listener's agreement.

1. Kono seetaa wa doo desu ka?

_____

2. Mizu wa doo desu ka?

_____

3. Nihongo no sensei wa doo desu ka?

_____

4. Shiken wa doo deshita ka?

_____

5. Kono jisho wa doo desu ka?

_____

6. Ano uchi wa doo desu ka?

_____

7. Ano konpyuuta wa doo deshita ka?

_____

8. Anata no heya wa doo desu ka?

_____

9. Tookyoo no natsu wa doo desu ka?

_____

10. Shigoto wa doo desu ka?

_____

The plain form of **-sugimasu** is **-sugiru**. You must use this form of **-sugimasu** if you want to express an opinion or belief about something. For example, _I think that the coffee is too hot:_

Koohii wa **atsusugiru** to omoimasu.

The plain form is also used in the pattern, _He, I, etc. said that the coffee was too hot:_

Koohii wa **atsusugiru** _to_ iimashita.

Do the following exercise using either of the above two patterns and the plain form of **-sugiru.**

1. I think that it's too far.

_____

2. He said that the beer was too cold.

_____

3. I think that the test is too easy.

_____

4. I said that the sweater was too small.

_____

5. I think that Hokkaido is too cold.

_____

6. They said that the shoes were too expensive.

_____

7. I think that the dictionary is too old.

_____

8. She said that the medicine was too strong.

_____

9. I think that the house is too far.

_____

10. We said that the train was too slow.

_____

26. OTHER EXPRESSIONS USING ADJECTIVES

Now we come to the use of *adjectival phrases* in Japanese. An adjectival phrase is simply a sentence using an adjective which then modifies another noun. For example:

Atama ga ii = (I, He, She, etc.) is intelligent.

Atama means *head*, so this sentence, literally translated, means that (somebody's) head is good. The entire expression **atama ga ii** forms an adjectival phrase meaning *intelligent* in English.

As a phrase, it can modify a noun.

Example: atama ga ii hito = an intelligent person
kimochi ga ii hi = a pleasant day

To say *He is an intelligent person,* all you need to do is add the word **desu** to the end of the phrase:

Atama ga ii hito desu.

Other commonly used adjectival phrases are:

me ga ookii	=	(eyes are big)
kuchi ga chiisai	=	(mouth is small)
ashi ga hayai	=	(walks fast)
sei ga takai	=	tall
sei ga hikui	=	short
kuchi ga warui	=	sharp tongued
hana ga takai	=	proud
kimochi ga ii	=	pleasant
kimochi ga warui	=	nauseating, disgusting
ki ga ookii	=	broad-minded
ki ga chiisai	=	petty
mimi ga tooi	=	hard of hearing

Referring to the list above, describe the following situations. Be sure to make a complete sentence by adding **desu** after the noun.

1. a person who doesn't quibble about small matters

_____

2. a person who doesn't mince words

_____

3. a pro basketball player

_____

4. a beautiful day in spring

_____

5. a person who cannot hear well

_____

6. a person who walks with his nose in the air

_____

7. a child with an IQ of 200

_____

8. a person who gets hung up on details

_____

9. a person who can walk a mile in a minute

_____

10. a movie filled with blood and gore

_____

In order to describe a place or a person in Japanese, the following construction is often used. Pay particular attention to the use of the particles **wa** and **ga**.

Tanaka-san **wa** atama **ga** ii desu. = Mr. Tanaka is intelligent.

Tookyoo **wa** hito **ga** ooi desu. = Tokyo is populous.

The **wa** particle indicates the person, place or thing being described while the **ga** particle is used in the adjectival phrase describing a feature or characteristic.

Translate these sentences into Japanese:

1. My mother has big eyes.

_____

2. Today is a pleasant day.

_____

3. My friend is hard of hearing.

_____

4. That actress has a small mouth.

_____

5. The teacher tells it like it is.

_____

6. Tomoko is tall.

_____

7. Akira is very intelligent.

_____

8. Mr. Tanaka is broad-minded.

_____

9. This room is pleasant.

_____

10. Mr. Matsuyama frets about small matters.

_____

Donna means *what kind.* **Donna hito desu ka?** means *What kind of person is he/she?*

Answer the following questions using one of the expressions you just practiced, or try making one up yourself. There is no need to repeat the subject.

1. Anata wa donna hito desu ka?

_____

2. Tomodachi wa donna hito desu ka?

_____

3. Kyoo wa doo desu ka?

_____

4. Nihongo no sensei wa donna hito desu ka?

_____

5. Maikeru Joodan wa donna hito desu ka?

_____

6. Anata no okaasan wa donna hito desu ka?

_____

27. Ooi and Sukunai

Two adjectives, **ooi** and **sukunai**, are unusual, and will be treated separately. Unlike other adjectives that you have studied so far, these two can be found only in the predicate. They never modify a noun in their *dictionary* form.

Ooi means *many, much, numerous, a lot,* etc. and can be used when you are talking about both countable and non-countable nouns. For example:

Hito ga ooi desu.	=	There are many people.
Mizu ga ooi desu.	=	There is a lot of water.

People is a countable noun because you can say one person, two people, etc. *Water* on the other hand is non-countable, as you cannot say one water, two waters.

Sukunai means *not many, not much, few, scarce,* etc. Like **ooi**, it can be used for both countable and non-countable nouns. For example:

Hito ga sukunai desu.	=	There are few people.
Tabemono ga sukunai desu.	=	There is little to eat.
		(Literally, "food is not much.")

Both **ooi** and **sukunai** can be inflected like any other adjective.

The **-soo** form of **sukunai** is **suku*nasasoo*** (slightly irregular), although **sukunasoo** is also heard.

Study the following sentence:

Paatii ni hito ga ooi desu. = There are many people at the party.

Rewrite the above sentence using the different forms you have already studied, as follows:

1. . . . were many . . . (formal)

2. . . . aren't many . . . (formal)

3. . . . weren't many . . . (Goldilocks)

_____

4. . . . has to be many . . .

_____

5. My friend said there are many . . .

_____

6. It's OK if there are many . . .

_____

7. There probably weren't many . . .

_____

8. I think there aren't many . . .

_____

9. There are many . . . , right?

_____

10. There were many . . . and so it was fun.

_____

Memorize the following sentence:

Paatii ni tabemono ga sukunai desu. = There is little food at the party.

Rewrite the above sentence using the forms and constructions you have studied.

1. There was . . . (plain)

_____

2. There wasn't . . . (Goldilocks)

_____

3. There isn't . . . (formal)

_____

4. I think that . . .

_____

5. My friend said that . . .

_____

6. There is . . . , right ?

_____

7. I understand there was . . .

_____

8. It's OK if there is . . . (formal)

_____

9. There was little food at the party so it wasn't fun.

   _____

10. There appears to be . . .

   _____

Earlier we said that both of these adjectives never modify nouns in their dictionary forms. This is absolutely true of **sukunai**. However, it is interesting to note that the noun form of **ooi**, **ooku** (a noun, oddly enough, although it looks like the **-ku** adjective form) can be used to describe nouns as in:

ooku **no** hito = many people

The word **ooku** is a formal word and is used when discussing topics of some import. Therefore, you are advised for the moment to use **ooku** to describe *people* or specific *places* managed by people, such as countries, companies, houses, or places of worship. Inanimate objects, animals, and abstract nouns are not usually modified by **ooku** in casual conversation, but can be modified by **takusan,** meaning many, a lot of, etc. Both **ooku** and **takusan** must be followed by the particle **no** when describing a noun.

Write these phrases in Japanese:

1. many Japanese

   _____

2. a lot of books

   _____

3. many countries

   _____

4. many towns

   _____

5. a lot of cats

   _____

6. a lot of students

   _____

7. many colleges

   _____

8. many novels

   _____

9. many teachers

_____

10. many children

_____

11. many pencils

_____

12. a lot of people

_____

28. "It's better if it's . . ."

Adjectives may also be used in the following construction:

[adj.] **hoo ga ii** (desu) = It's better if it's [adj.]

Because of the use of the word *if* in English, the temptation would be to use the conditional **-ba** form. However, in Japanese, **hoo ga ii** indicates a comparison rather than a conditional. The sentence **akai hoo ga ii desu** means *It's better if it's red* (as compared to another color).

Look at the following examples:

Biiru wa tsumetai *hoo ga ii* desu. = Beer is better if it's cold.

Biiru wa tsumetaku nai *hoo ga ii*. = Beer is better if it's not cold.

As you can see, the plain present or negative form of the adjective may be used before **hoo ga ii**. The past tense of adjectives is not used before **hoo ga ii**. The level of politeness is determined by **ii** or **ii desu**.

Express the following in Japanese:

1. It's better if it's new.

2. It's better if it's not cheap.

3. Coffee is better if it's hot.

4. Computers are better if they're new.

5. Dictionaries are better if they're not old.

6. Expensive shoes are better. (Shoes are better if they're expensive.)

7. Curry rice is better if it's spicy.

8. Sake is better if it's hot.

_____

9. Detailed explanations are better.

_____

10. Teachers are better if they're not strict.

_____

11. It's better if the food is unusual.

_____

12. Small houses are better.

_____

In the following exercise, answer the questions using the **hoo ga ii desu** pattern and an appropriate adjective in the present or negative plain form as required:

Example: Kutsu wa akakute mo ii desu ka? = Is it OK if the shoes are red?
Iie. Akaku nai hoo ga ii desu. = No. It's better if they are not red.

OR

Iie. Kuroi hoo ga ii desu. = No. It's better if they're black.

1. Seetaa wa ookikute mo ii desu ka?
Iie. _____

2. Jisho wa furukute mo ii desu ka?
Iie. _____

3. Mondai wa yasashikute mo ii desu ka?
Iie. _____

4. Uchi wa chiisakute mo ii desu ka?
Iie. _____

5. Sensei wa kibishiku nakute mo ii desu ka?
Iie. _____

6. Suupu wa atsuku nakute mo ii desu ka?
Iie. _____

7. Jikan wa osokute mo ii desu ka?
   Iie. _____

8. Gakkoo wa chikaku nakute mo ii desu ka?
   Iie. _____

9. Suutsu wa kuroku nakute mo ii desu ka?
   Iie. _____

10. Setsumei wa kuwashikute mo ii desu ka?
    Iie. _____

Other adjectives may be used after **hoo ga** to get different meanings. For example:

. . . hoo ga oishii desu	=	It tastes better if . . .
. . . hoo ga omoshiroi desu	=	It's more interesting if . . .

Another commonly used pattern is . . . **hoo ga suki desu** (*I prefer* . . .).

What do the following sentences mean?

1. Koohii wa atsui hoo ga oishii desu.
   _____

2. Eiga wa furui hoo ga omoshiroi desu.
   _____

3. Biiru wa tsumetai hoo ga suki desu.
   _____

4. Biiru wa anmari tsumetaku nai hoo ga suki desu.
   _____

5. Kuruma wa chiisai hoo ga suki desu.
   _____

6. Sashimi wa atarashii hoo ga oishii desu.
   _____

7. Konpyuuta wa atarashii hoo ga takai desu.
   _____

8. Karee raisu wa anmari karaku nai hoo ga oishii desu.
   _____

Try translating these sentences, using the above exercise as a reference.

1. Juice tastes better if it's cold.

2. Problems are more interesting if they're difficult.

3. I prefer big cars.

4. I prefer large sweaters.

5. Cakes taste better if they are not sweet.

6. Japanese tea tastes better if it's hot.

7. Old houses are more interesting.

8. Vegetables taste better if they are fresh.

9. New cars are more expensive.

10. Books are more interesting if they're old.

11. I prefer hot rice.

12. Soup tastes better if it's hot.

29. Tooi and Chikai

The adjectives **tooi** (far away) and **chikai** (nearby) operate like any other adjective when used in the predicate. However, when they are the only modifier of a noun indicating a specific place, they are used in their **-ku** form with the particle **no**.

A park that is far away is **tooku no kooen** and a school that is nearby is **chikaku no gakkoo**. Both the words **tooku** and **chikaku** are nouns and should not be confused with the adverbial **-ku** form. **Tooku** and **chikaku** may be used by themselves (not modifying a noun) as in:

Tooku e ikimashita. = We went far.
Kono chikaku de kaimashita. = We bought it around here.

Fortunately, there are only a few adjectives in Japanese which use the **-ku** form as nouns. Other ones that follow that form are **ooi**, which has already been studied, and **hayai** and **osoi**, which also have noun forms.

There are three exceptions to the use of **tooku no** and **chikaku no,** in which the particle **no** is omitted:

1) The word **tokoro** meaning place is modified by **tooi** and **chikai**.
2) When linking adjectives using the **-te** form of **chikai** or **tooi**.
   Example: chikakute ii gakkoo = a good school nearby
           tookute abunai kooen = a dangerous park faraway
3) when using an adverb to modify **chikai** and **tooi** such as **totemo** or **amari**.
   Example: totemo chikai resutoran = a restaurant that is very close

Keeping the above explanations in mind, write the following phrases and sentences in Japanese. Your first thought should be whether the adjectives are modifying a noun or are in the predicate.

1. a school faraway

   _____

2. someplace nearby

   _____

3. a coffee shop which is nearby and good

   _____

4. some place far away

   _____

5. That hospital is small and far away.

   _____

6. a college which is nearby

   _____

7. a library which is far away

   _____

8. That department store is far away but it's good.

   _____

9. We went some place near.

   _____

10. We went to a restaurant that is nearby and delicious.

    _____

11. a supermarket that's not very far

    _____

12. It's better if it's near.

    _____

13. We went to a park that is very near.

    _____

14. It's OK if the restaurant is not near.

    _____

15. The school has to be near.

    _____

16. It's better if it's not far.

    _____

17. A place nearby would be good.

    _____

18. We saw it near here.

    _____

PART II

NA ADJECTIVES

1. THE NA ADJECTIVE

There is another group of describing words which are sometimes called adjectival nominatives or adjectival nominals. As these important sounding names imply, these words are half adjective, half noun. They are like adjectives because they modify nouns. However, grammatically, these adjectives behave more like nouns. In other words, they are treated differently from the adjectives you have just studied. For the sake of brevity, these words will be called *na* adjectives. The reason for the **na** will be explained later.

Here is a list of common *na* adjectives we will be working with.

na *adjective*	*Meaning*
anzen	safe
benri	convenient, handy
fuben	inconvenient, not handy
genki	healthy, energetic
kirei	pretty, clean
suteki	chic, attractive, nifty
dame	no good, broken
shinsetsu	kind, considerate
hen	strange, weird
yuumei	famous
teinei	polite
shitsurei	rude
tekitoo	appropriate, suitable, fitting
rippa	magnificent, splendid, fine
modan	modern
hansamu	handsome, good looking (men only)
iroiro	various
daijoobu	fine, OK, no problem
shizuka	quiet
raku	comfortable
joohin	refined, elegant
majime	serious-minded, diligent
taisetsu	important, valuable, precious
baka	stupid
nigiyaka	bustling, lively

taikutsu	boring, bored
hima	having free time

Referring to the list above, find a **na** adjective that describes the following situations (More than one of the above can be correct):

1. a pair of slacks with an elastic waist
   _____

2. a tidy room
   _____

3. snow in August
   _____

4. a store clerk who throws the change in your face
   _____

5. Mel Gibson
   _____

6. a person who helps an old woman cross the street
   _____

7. a futuristic skyscraper
   _____

8. the teddy bear you can't sleep without
   _____

9. a pocketknife with scissors, bottle opener, toenail cutter, back scratcher
   _____

10. a country road at night
    _____

11. a co-worker who sits all day twiddling his thumbs
    _____

12. a house located an hour away from the nearest store
    _____

13. a telephone with no dial tone
    _____

14. the newest "in" sweater
    _____

15. someone who keeps his nose to the grindstone
    _____

16. a book with just the explanations you're looking for
    _____

17. a car with seat belts, air bags and built like a vault
    _____

18. Times Square on New Year's Eve
   _____

19. a person with regal bearing
   _____

20. a person who says "please" and "thank you"
   _____

21. yourself
   _____
   _____

It is necessary for you to be able to distinguish between **na** adjectives and _regular_ adjectives. In the exercise below write **na** if the word is a **na** adjective or **i** if the word is a _regular_ adjective. Write the meaning in the space provided in either case.

1. nigiyaka > na? i?
   Meaning: _____

2. benri >
   _____

3. mezurashii >
   _____

4. genki >
   _____

5. shinsetsu >
   _____

6. hima >
   _____

7. yuumei >
   _____

8. sutcki >
   _____

9. ii >
   _____

10. baka >
_____

11. sugoi >
_____

12. aoi >
_____

13. anzen >
_____

14. iroiro >
_____

15. raku >
_____

16. taikutsu >
_____

17. shizuka >
_____

18. fuben >
_____

19. tekitoo >
_____

20. joohin >
_____

In the following exercise, write an adjective which is *opposite* in meaning (either a **na** adjective or a *regular* adjective).

1. nigiyaka _____

2. taikutsu _____

3. fuben _____

4. hima _____

5. dame _____

6. anzen _____

7. kirei _____

8. shitsurei _____

Fill in the missing letters of these **na** adjectives and give their respective meanings:

1. h__n = _____

2. s__ __zuk__ = _____

3. da__jo__bu = _____

4. __roi__o = _____

5. yu__m__i = _____

6. __aka = _____

7. t__ise__su = _____

8. g__n__i = _____

9. t__k__to__ = _____

10. r__ __pa = _____

11. __im__ = _____

12. m__jim__ = _____

2. THE NA ADJECTIVE IN THE PREDICATE: NON-PAST AFFIRMATIVE

In order to make a complete sentence, **na** adjectives must be followed by **desu** or one of its forms. Unlike with *regular* adjectives, you cannot use a **na** adjective by itself and have a complete sentence. **Atsui** is a complete sentence meaning *it's hot,* but **kirei** by itself is not a sentence.

The formal way of saying *It is clean* is **Kirei desu.**

Write the formal forms for the following sentences (Remember that you don't need to translate subject pronouns such as *I, we, you, he, she, they,* or *it*):

1. He's kind. _____

2. I'm bored. _____

3. I'm OK. _____

4. It's quiet. _____

5. It's handy. _____

6. It's inconvenient. _____

7. It's safe. _____

8. I'm free (I have free time). _____

9. It's splendid. _____

10. She's attractive. _____

11. It's modern. _____

12. It's appropriate. _____

13. It's important. _____

14. It's comfortable. _____

15. He's polite. _____

16. It's convenient. _____

17. It's lively. _____

18. It's broken. _____

19. It's strange. _____

20. She's famous. _____

The plain way of saying *It's clean/pretty* is **Kirei da.** As you can guess, **da** is the plain form of **desu**. Compare the plain forms of **na** adjectives and *regular* adjectives:

> Regular adjective: atsui
> **Na** adjective: kirei da

In the following exercise, write the plain form of the sentence. You will find some *regular* adjectives and some **na** adjectives so be sure to give the correct form as in the example above.

1. Shizuka desu. > _____

2. Ookii desu. > _____

3. Isogashii desu. > _____

4. Yuumei desu. > _____

5. Taisetsu desu. > _____

6. Shitsurei desu. > _____

7. Tanoshii desu. > _____

8. Genki desu. > _____

9. Teinei desu. > _____

10. Daijoobu desu. > _____

11. Anzen desu. > _____

12. Suzushii desu. > _____

13. Kuroi desu. > _____

14. Hima desu. > _____

15. Dame desu. > _____

16. Tekitoo desu.> _____

17. Takai desu. > _____

18. Tooi desu. > _____

19. Baka desu. > _____

20. Suteki desu. > _____

THE NA ADJECTIVE IN THE PREDICATE: NON-PAST NEGATIVE

The negative of **Kirei desu** is **Kirei ja arimasen,** *It is not clean/pretty.* **Dewa arimasen** is the negative formal form of **desu.** In conversation, **ja arimasen** (the level is still formal) is often used and has the same meaning as **dewa arimasen**. Do not make the common mistake in thinking that **arimasen** by itself is the negative of **desu!**

Write these sentences below in the formal *negative* form. Use appropriate adverbs where required.

1. I'm not bored.

_____

2. She's not very attractive.

   _____

3. It's not lively at all.

   _____

4. He's not very handsome.

   _____

5. She's not very polite.

   _____

6. Tokyo is not very quiet.

   _____

7. The doctor is not very kind.

   _____

8. The telephone isn't broken.

   _____

9. The sweater isn't very chic.

   _____

10. The school isn't safe.

   _____

11. The movie is not boring at all.

   _____

12. Mother isn't very well (healthy).

   _____

13. The woman isn't refined.

   _____

14. The room is not clean.

   _____

15. I don't have free time.

   _____

The plain form of **ja arimasen** is **ja nai**. You may also use **dewa nai** for the negative non-past plain form.

   Example: Kirei **ja arimasen.** > Kirei **ja nai.**

Both of the above sentences mean *It is not clean*. The only difference is the level of formality or politeness. Keep in mind that the negative plain form of *regular* adjectives is the **-ku nai** as in **atsuku nai**.

Give the *negative plain* form of the following. You will find some of them to be **na** adjectives and some will be regular adjectives, so be sure to inflect them in the correct manner.

1. muzukashii desu > _____

2. majime desu > _____

3. shitsurei desu > _____

4. yasui desu > _____

5. taisetsu desu > _____

6. rippa desu > _____

7. fuben desu > _____

8. modan desu > _____

9. samui desu > _____

10. teinei desu > _____

11. shizuka desu > _____

12. suteki desu > _____

13. tekitoo desu > _____

14. raku desu > _____

15. suzushii desu > _____

16. ii desu > _____

17. taisetsu desu > _____

18. hima desu > _____

19. daijoobu desu > _____

20. atarashii desu > _____

Circle the choice that will make a correct sentence.

1. Uchi wa (benri ja nai, benri nai).

2. Uchi wa (tooku ja nai, tooku nai).

3. Sensei wa (shinsetsu, shinsetsu da).

4. Toire wa (kireku nai, kirei dewa nai).

5. Shiken wa (muzukashiku nai, muzukashii ja nai).

6. Koko wa (shizuku nai, shizuka ja arimasen).

7. Denwa wa (dame desu, dame arimasen).

8. Tookyoo wa (nigiyaka da, nigiyaka nai).

9. Eiga wa (omoshiroi da, omoshiroi).

10. Kono biru wa (modan, modan da).

THE NA ADJECTIVE IN THE PREDICATE: AFFIRMATIVE PAST

The past tense of **desu** is **deshita**. Therefore, to arrive at the formal level of the past affirmative, all you need to do is to add **deshita** to the **na** adjective.

Example: Kirei deshita. = It was pretty.

Notice that unlike *regular* adjectives, the **na** adjective is not inflected.

Review the formal affirmative past tense of *regular* adjectives and do the following exercise.

1. It was boring. _____

2. It was warm. _____

3. It was OK. _____

4. He was handsome. _____

5. It was famous. _____

6. I was lonely. _____

7. It was delicious. _____

8. It was safe. _____

9. He was strange. _____

10. It was dangerous. _____

11. It was inconvenient. _____

12. It was appropriate. _____

13. She was polite. _____

14. I had free time. _____

15. It was comfortable. _____

16. He was serious-minded. _____

17. It was lively. _____

18. It was no good. _____

19. It was clean. _____

20. She was attractive. _____

The plain form of **deshita** is **datta**. In order to say **kirei deshita** in a friendlier way, you would say **kirei datta.**

Give the *past tense* of the following according to the level indicated in parentheses. Again, *regular* adjectives are mixed in the drill.

1. raku (formal) _____

2. shizuka (plain) _____

3. yuumei (plain) _____

4. samui (formal) _____

5. mezurashii (plain) _____

6. daijoobu (formal) _____

7. hima (plain) _____

8. taikutsu (formal) _____

9. tekitoo (plain) _____

10. joohin (formal) _____

11. baka (plain) _____

12. anzen (formal) _____

13. nigiyaka (formal) _____

14. hansamu (plain) _____

15. rippa (plain) _____

16. teinei (formal) _____

17. hayai (plain) _____

18. modan (formal) _____

19. genki (plain) _____

20. iroiro (formal) _____

THE NA ADJECTIVE IN THE PREDICATE: PAST NEGATIVE

The formal past negative of **desu** is **ja arimasen deshita** or **dewa arimasen deshita.** *Ja arimasen deshita* is commonly used in conversation. Therefore:

Kirei ja arimasen deshita. = It was not clean/pretty.

Compare this ending to the **-ku arimasen deshita** form of *regular* adjectives. By now, you should have noticed that **na** adjectives are constants; they themselves are *never* changed.

Do this exercise. You can think of this as a linguistic mixed drill, as both types of adjectives will appear.

1. It wasn't quiet. _____

2. They weren't handsome. _____

3. They weren't expensive. _____

4. It wasn't chic. _____

5. It wasn't appropriate. _____

6. It wasn't comfortable. _____

7. She wasn't rude. _____

8. It wasn't hot. _____

9. I wasn't busy. _____

10. I didn't have free time. _____

11. He wasn't polite. _____

12. It wasn't boring. _____

13. It wasn't interesting. _____

14. He wasn't famous. _____

15. It wasn't convenient. _____

16. They weren't refined. _____

17. I wasn't stupid. _____

18. It wasn't broken. _____

19. It wasn't near. _____

20. It wasn't magnificent. _____

Of course, there is a plain form of the past negative tense, which is **ja nakatta** or **dewa nakatta**.

> Example: Kirei ja arimasen deshita. = Kirei ja nakatta.
> = It was not pretty/clean.

Again, compare **ja nakatta** to the **-ku nakatta** form used to inflect adjectives to the negative past plain tense.

Do this mixed drill exercise using the plain form of the adjective.

1. yasashii > _____

2. shinsetsu > _____

3. taisetsu > _____

4. benri > _____

5. teinei > _____

6. tanoshii > _____

7. nigiyaka > _____

8. yuumei > _____

9. fuben > _____

10. suteki > _____

11. genki > _____

12. ii > _____

13. raku > _____

14. taikutsu > _____

15. majime > _____

3. GOLDILOCKS AND THE NA ADJECTIVE

The Goldilocks level can also be used with **na** adjectives. As with *regular* adjectives, it can only be used with **na** adjectives in their *negative* forms, both past and non-past.

As with *regular* adjectives, the word **desu** is added to the plain negative forms to create an intermediate level between formal and informal. Thus:

Kirei ja nai. = **Kirei ja nai desu.** = Kirei ja arimasen.

Kirei ja nakatta. = **Kirei ja nakatta desu.** = Kirei ja arimasen deshita.

Change the following formal forms to the Goldilocks form:

1. Taisetsu ja arimasen. > _____

2. Benri ja arimasen deshita. > _____

3. Kirei ja arimasen. > _____

4. Yasuku arimasen. > _____

5. Tooku arimasen. > _____

6. Shizuka ja arimasen deshita. > _____

7. Tekitoo ja arimasen. > _____

8. Yuumei ja arimasen deshita. > _____

9. Suteki ja arimasen. > _____

10. Rippa ja arimasen deshita. > _____

11. Chiisaku arimasen. > _____

12. Genki ja arimasen. > _____

13. Raku ja arimasen deshita. > _____

14. Nigiyaka ja arimasen. > _____

15. Anzen ja arimasen. > _____

4. REVIEW OF BASIC INFLECTIONS

Express each adjective below at the level of formality indicated. Inflect tense as appropriate.

shizuka
1. It's not (formal) _____
2. It is (plain) _____
3. It was (formal) _____
4. It wasn't (Goldilocks) _____

oishii
1. It is (plain) _____
2. It's not (formal) _____
3. It wasn't (plain) _____
4. It was (formal) _____

dame
1. It wasn't (Goldilocks)_____
2. It was (formal) _____
3. It isn't (plain) _____
4. It is (plain) _____

tekitoo
1. It is (formal) _____
2. It isn't (plain) _____
3. It was (plain) _____
4. It wasn't (formal) _____

taisetsu
1. It was (formal) _____
2. It isn't (Goldilocks) _____
3. It was (formal) _____
4. It wasn't (formal) _____

Find the errors in the following sentences and rewrite them correctly:

1. Tookyoo wa shizuku nakatta desu.

   _____

2. Kono uchi wa benri datta desu.

   _____

3. Kyoo wa atsui deshita.

   _____

4. Sono isha wa shinsetsu ja nakatta deshita.

   _____

5. Watashi wa baka arimasen.

   _____

5. NA ADJECTIVES WHEN THEY DESCRIBE A NOUN

So far, we have seen cases where **na** adjectives are used in the predicate. Here, we will examine how **na** adjectives can be used to describe nouns. In English, such examples would include *a* quiet *man, a* kind *professor, a* convenient *location.*

Remember, in the case of *regular* adjectives, the adjective is placed directly before the noun with no intervening particle.

> Example: atsui koohii

In the case of **na** adjectives, the particle **na** must be inserted between the adjective and the noun. Voila! the reason for the appellation "**na** adjective"!

> Example: kirei **na** hito, shizuka **na** resutoran

Here are some more nouns we will use for the exercises to follow:

Noun	Meaning
kuni	country
isha	doctor, physician
kangofu	nurse
machi	town, city
mise	store
tokoro	place, locale
gakusei	student
tekisuto	text
ten-in	store clerk
tokei	clock, watch
hi	day

How would you express the following phrases in Japanese? Watch out for *regular* adjectives:

1. a quiet town _____

2. a kind nurse _____

3. a strange day _____

4. a busy person _____

5. a person with free time _____

6. a fine person _____

7. a valuable watch _____

8. an appropriate text _____

9. a hot day _____

10. a boring movie _____

11. a rude store clerk _____

12. a polite student _____

14. various newspapers _____

15. a large country _____

16. a comfortable sweater _____

17. a safe place _____

18. a dangerous place _____

19. a famous doctor _____

20. a strict teacher _____

21. a handy telephone _____

22. a serious student _____

23. a lively town _____

24. a stupid student _____

25. a refined person _____

One way to make these phrases into complete sentences would be to add **desu** or one of its forms.

Example: Fuben na uchi deshita. = It was an inconvenient house.

However, as this is probably too easy for you at this point, let's use the pattern *there is* or *there are*. In Japanese, if you want to state the existence of an *inanimate* object, you would say for example:

Hon ga arimasu. = There is a book. / There are books.

If you were speaking of an *animate* object such as a person or animal, you would say for example:

Shizuka na hito ga imasu. = There is a quiet person. /
There are quiet people.

Both **arimasu** and **imasu** are formal expressions. In this pattern, the particle that shows what exists is **ga**.

Translate the following sentences into Japanese:

1. There are kind doctors.
   _____

2. There are interesting movies.
   _____

3. There are appropriate texts.
   _____

4. There are valuable clocks.
   _____

5. There are attractive women.
   _____

6. There is hot coffee.
   _____

7. There are modern buildings.

   _____

8. There are convenient stores.

   _____

9. There are handsome men.

   _____

10. There are various people.

    _____

11. There are bustling cities.

    _____

12. There are quiet parks.

    _____

13. There are polite store clerks.

    _____

14. There are safe places.

    _____

15. There are good students.

    _____

Modify the nouns with the adjectives indicated. Write out the entire sentence.

. . . **eiga** o mimashita = I saw a . . . movie.

1. I saw an interesting movie. > _____

2. boring > _____

3. old > _____

. . . **hito** ni aimashita = I met (a/an) . . . person

1. famous > _____

2. kind > _____

3. good > _____

4. attractive >) _____

... **shoosetsu** o yomimashita = I read (a/an) ... novel.

1. boring > _____

2. appropriate > _____

3. new > _____

4. various > _____

... **tokei** o kaimashita = I bought (a/an) ... watch.

1. expensive > _____

2. pretty > _____

3. various > _____

4. attractive > _____

... **koto** o iimashita = I said ... things

1. stupid > _____

2. bad > _____

3. strange > _____

4. rude > _____

6. SUKI/KIRAI, JOOZU/HETA

These four **na** adjectives, **suki**, **kirai**, **joozu**, and **heta**, are introduced separately from the others, as these sometimes require an "object."

Suki desu.	=	I like it.
Kirai desu.	=	I dislike it. (I hate it.)
Joozu desu.	=	He's good at it.
Heta desu.	=	They're bad at it.

If you want to say *I like sushi,* you would say **Sushi ga suki desu.** Many students are tempted to say **Sushi o suki desu,** believing that sushi is the direct object of **suki desu.** Generally speaking, you will use the particle **o** only with *verbs*. The above four **na** adjectives are not verbs and so require either the particle **ga** or **wa** for the thing(s) one likes, dislikes, is good at, or is bad at. In affirmative sentences, usually the particle **ga** is used. In negative sentences, usually **wa** is used.

The words **kirai** and **heta** have strong meanings, so be careful when you use them. Telling the boss's wife 'Tempura ga kirai desu,' after she has labored in a hot kitchen to make it will not earn you Brownie points! In the same vein, my advice is to say 'heta desu' only when speaking about your own abilities.

Using the formal level, write an equivalent sentence in Japanese.

1. I like beer.

   _____

2. I don't like tempura.

   _____

3. I dislike tennis.

   _____

4. He's very good at tennis.

   _____

5. I don't play tennis well.

   _____

6. I don't like tempura very much.

   _____

7. He was good at tennis.

   _____

8. He wasn't bad at tennis.

   _____

9. I don't dislike coffee.

   _____

10. I'm bad at tennis.

    _____

The person who likes, dislikes, is good at, or is bad at is generally marked by the particle **wa.**

> Example: Tanaka-san **wa** tenisu **ga** joozu desu.
> Tanaka-san **wa** tenisu **wa** joozu ja arimasen.

Try these sentences:

1. Do you (anata) like soup ?

   _____

2. My friend is good at golf.

   _____

3. Haruko isn't good at Spanish.

   _____

4. My mom is a good cook (good at cooking).

   _____

5. I [watashi] am not very good at piano.

   _____

6. Mr. Suzuki speaks English well (is very good at English).

   _____

7. My father is not bad at golf.

   _____

When these **na** adjectives modify nouns, they of course require the use of the particle **na** preceding the noun they modify.

> Example: suki na keeki   =   the cake *that I like*
> kirai na keeki   =   the cake *that I hate*

joozu na eigo   =   proficient English
heta na eigo   =   bad (broken) English

Describe the following situations with one of the above **na** adjectives.

    Example: carrot cake > suki na keeki

1. pidgin English > _____

2. a golf shot that lands in a bunker > _____

3. chocolate mousse cake > _____

4. a service ace in tennis > _____

5. a person you try to avoid > _____

6. unagi (broiled eel) zushi > _____

7. fluent Japanese > _____

8. clam chowder > _____

9. a banging piano sound > _____

10. your favorite teacher > _____

The word **deshoo** meaning *probably* which was studied in the previous section is often used with **suki** and **kirai** to speak of someone else's likes and dislikes. Of course, it can be used with any of the **na** adjectives, but let's practice it here with the **na** adjectives introduced in this section.

With **na** adjectives, **deshoo** can be added to the adjective directly in the non-past affirmative.

    Example: Mr. Tanaka probably likes it. = Tanaka-san wa suki deshoo.

With other forms, **deshoo** follows the plain form.

Example: Mr. Tanaka probably didn't like it. = Tanaka-san wa suki ja
           nakatta deshoo.

Express the following in Japanese :

1. Ms. Yamamoto probably likes sake.
    _____

2. The student is probably good at English.
    _____

3. Mr. Ohta probably isn't good at Spanish.
    _____

4. The teacher probably hated it.
    _____

5. Taroo probably liked the TV program.
    _____

6. My mother probably won't like the cake.
    _____

7. That person probably wasn't good at piano.
    _____

8. Ms. Takahashi probably liked the tempura.
    _____

7. THE NA ADJECTIVE AS ADVERB

You learned in the previous section that when you modify a verb with a *regular* adjective, you must change the adjective to its **-ku** form.

To use a **na** adjective to modify a verb, all you have to do is add the particle **ni** to it.

Example: shinsetsu ni = kindly

Give the adverb form of the following adjectives:

1. benri > _____

2. utsukushii > _____

3. anzen > _____

4. genki > _____

5. mezurashii > _____

6. tooi > _____

7. suteki > _____

8. rippa > _____

9. fuben > _____

10. tsuyoi > _____

Modifying the verb **narimashita** (*to become*), write these sentences in Japanese using the adverb form of the appropriate adjective:

Example: The store clerk became polite. = Ten-in wa teinei ni narimashita.

1. The school became safe.

   _____

2. The school became dangerous.

   _____

3. The room got clean.

   _____

4. The room got dirty.

   _____

5. The restaurant got quiet.

   _____

6. The restaurant became lively.

   _____

7. It became inconvenient.

   _____

8. The student became pretty.

   _____

9. He became healthy.

   _____

10. The doctor became famous.

   _____

In the previous section, we used the adverb form of *regular* adjectives and **shimasu** to make sentences meaning *Someone makes something big, cheap, easy, etc.* Here, let's use the polite command form of **shimasu, shite kudasai** to tell someone to *Please make it _____.*

Example: Shizuka ni shite kudasai. = Please make [yourself] quiet.
           (Please be quiet.)

1. Please clean it (make it clean).

   _____

2. Please make it convenient.

   _____

3. Please make it polite.

   _____

4. Please make it cheap.

   _____

5. Please make yourself comfortable.

   _____

6. Please make it fast.

_____

7. Please make it red.

_____

8. Please make it safe.

_____

Study this list of verbs:

kotaemashita	answered
unten shimashita	drove (a vehicle)
oshiemashita	told, taught
mimashita	saw, watched, examined
sakimashita	bloomed

Using the above list and the verbs that have been introduced earlier, write the English equivalent of the following sentences:

1. Kodomo wa genki ni asobimashita.

_____

2. Ten-in wa teinei ni kotaemashita.

_____

3. Isha wa shinsetsu ni mimashita.

_____

4. Gakusei wa majime ni kotaemashita.

_____

5. Kuruma o anzen ni unten shimashita.

_____

6. Machi wa modan ni narimashita.

_____

7. Sensei wa joozu ni oshiemashita.

_____

8. Hana ga kirei ni sakimashita.

_____

8. LINKING NA ADJECTIVES

As with *regular* adjectives, it is possible to link a **na** adjective to another **na** adjective or to another *regular* adjective.

With *regular* adjectives, you need to change the adjective to its **-kute** form. With **na** adjectives, all you need to do is add the **-te** form of **desu (de)**, to the **na** adjective. Therefore, **kirei de** is the equivalent **-kute** form for **na** adjectives.

To make the sentence *It is clean and inexpensive,* you would say:

Kirei de yasui desu.

Keep in mind that the **-te** form does not have a tense. The tense of the sentence is determined by the last inflected expression, be it **desu**, a *regular* adjective or a verb.

In the following exercise, first decide whether the word is a *regular* adjective or a **na** adjective, then give the appropriate **-te** form:

1. hen > _____

2. suteki > _____

3. abunai > _____

4. akai > _____

5. baka > _____

6. modan > _____

7. iroiro > _____

8. fuben > _____

9. teinei > _____

10. yasashii > _____

What do the following sentences mean in English?

1. Ano biru wa totemo modan de kirei desu.
    _____

2. Uchi wa tookute fuben desu.
    _____

3. Ano hito wa teinei de joohin desu.
    _____

4. Ano okashi wa kirei de oishikatta desu.
    _____

5. Sono mise wa chiisakute benri ja arimasen.
    _____

6. Ano hito wa baka de shinsetsu ja arimasen.
    _____

7. Ano resutoran wa shizuka de totemo oishikatta desu.
    _____

8. Nihongo no kurasu wa nigiyaka de omoshiroi desu.
    _____

In this next exercise, describe the noun given with the two adjectives in parentheses. Write in complete sentences. If the first adjective is a *regular* adjective, you must link it to the **na** adjective by using the **-kute** form.

1. sensei (nice and kind)
    _____

2. isha (considerate, refined)
    _____

3. ten-in (young and pretty)
    _____

4. uchi (near and convenient)
    _____

5. gakkoo (small and safe)
    _____

Write an equivalent Japanese sentence for each of the following sentences. Be aware of the tense of each sentence.

1. The park is dirty and not safe.

2. The text was detailed and difficult.

3. The hotel was new and magnificent.

4. The store is nearby and convenient.

5. The park is quiet and pretty.

6. My friend is handsome and kind.

7. The library is large and convenient.

8. The team is strong and famous.

Like the **-kute** form, the **-te** form of adjectives can be used to add a clause to your sentence. Instead of saying **Ano machi wa fuben desu. Komarimashita,** you can make one sentence,

Ano machi wa fuben de komarimashita.   =   That town was inconvenient so
                                                                         I had problems.

As the example above shows, the **-te** form can indicate the reason for the second clause, **komarimashita.**

Using the **-te** form, combine the two sentences. Tell what each sentence means in English. You do not have to repeat the subject if it is the same for both clauses.

1. Ano eiga wa yuumei desu.
   Ano eiga wa omoshirokatta desu.

2. Ano depaato wa benri desu.
   Yoku ikimasu.

   _____

   _____

3. Ano sensei wa chotto hen desu.
   Watashi wa anmari hanashimasen.

   _____

   _____

4. Ano isha wa shinsetsu desu.
   Totemo suki desu.

   _____

   _____

5. Ano gakusei wa majime desu.
   Itsumo benkyoo shimasu.

   _____

   _____

6. Mise wa fuben desu.
   Komarimashita.

   _____

   _____

9. THE NEGATIVE -TE FORM OF NA ADJECTIVES

If you want to say in one sentence that a restaurant *is not quiet* and *is expensive,* you would need to use the **-te** form of the negative **shizuka ja arimasen**.

First, you get the plain negative form, **shizuka ja nai**, and then substitute **ja nakute** for **nai.**

> Example: shizuka ja arimasen > shizuka ja nai > shizuka ja nakute
> hen ja arimasen > hen ja nai > hen ja nakute

The negative **-te** form of **shizuka dewa arimasen** is **shizuka de nakute**. Notice that the **wa** is dropped in this form.

Contrast this form to the negative **-te** form of *regular* adjectives:

> **Example:** atsui > atsuku nai > atsuku nakute

Give the negative **-te** form of the following adjectives:

1. kirei > _____

2. kuroi > _____

3. anzen > _____

4. yuumei > _____

5. taisetsu > _____

6. majime > _____

7. ii > _____

8. hima > _____

9. taikutsu > _____

10. shitsurei > _____

11. suzushii > _____

12. genki > _____

13. osoi > _____

14. furui > _____

15. suteki > _____

Give an equivalent in Japanese for the following sentences. Keep the order of the adjectives the same as the English sentences. In some sentences, you will have to use the negative of *regular* adjectives.

1. The restaurant is *not* very pretty and is *not* good.
   _____

2. The computer is *not* new and is slow.
   _____

3. The sweater is *not* very expensive and is attractive.
   _____

4. That person is *not* kind and is forbidding.
   _____

5. This car is *not* big and is inconvenient.
   _____

In previous sections, you learned that the **-te** form can be used to connect clauses and that depending on the context, it can mean *and so*.

In this exercise, using the negative **-te** form of either **na** or *regular* adjectives, give two qualities about the thing when asked . . . **doo desu ka?** (*How is . . . ?*)

Example: Q. Kono kooen wa doo desu ka? = How is this park?
          A. Anzen ja nakute suki ja arimasen. = It is not safe and (so) I
             don't like it.

1. Ano resutoran wa doo desu ka?
   _____

2. Ano gakusei wa doo desu ka?

   _____

3. Kono eiga wa doo desu ka?

   _____

4. Nihongo no sensei wa doo desu ka?

   _____

5. Sono mise wa doo desu ka?

   _____

6. Ano kangofu wa doo desu ka?

   _____

7. Ano ten-in wa doo desu ka?

   _____

8. Koko wa doo desu ka?

   _____

9. Ano toshokan wa doo desu ka?

   _____

10. Kono kissaten wa doo desu ka?

    _____

As a final review, determine which adjective in Japanese would best express the one given in English. Some will be *regular* adjectives, others will be **na** adjectives. Give the appropriat*e* **-te** form of each. Give the negative **-te** form where indicated.

Example: quiet [and] = shizuka de
           not quiet [and] = shizuka ja nakute

1. healthy [and] = _____

2. safe [and] = _____

3. not comfortable [and] = _____

4. white [and] = _____

5. handsome [and] = _____

6. not kind [and] = _____

7. far [and] = _____

8. not near [and] = _____

9. attractive [and] = _____

10. valuable [and] = _____

11. not lively [and] = _____

12. not convenient [and] = _____

13. serious-minded [and] = _____

14. not fun [and] = _____

15. not modern [and] = _____

10. LINKING NA ADJECTIVES WHEN DESCRIBING A NOUN

Thus far, we have been linking adjectives in the predicate. Now let's use the **-te** form to describe a noun with two or more adjectives.

If you wanted to say *a convenient, large house,* you would use the **-te** form of **benri desu (benri de)** and add the *regular* adjective **ookii**:

benri de ookii uchi

There is no particle between the *regular* adjective **ookii** and the noun **uchi**.

However, if we switched the expression to *a large, convenient house,* you would need the **-te** form of **ookii (ookikute)**, and then you would add the **na** adjective **benri**:

ookikute *benri na* uchi

If you wanted to say *a convenient, safe house,* using two **na** adjectives, you would simply add the **na** adjective to **benri de**:

benri **de** anzen na uchi

In Japanese, generally adjectives which denote an attribute (*red, big, tall*) of an object or person are stated first. Adjectives which require subjective evaluation (*good, pretty, delicious*) usually follow.

Keeping the order of adjectives given, write these phrases:

1. a white, pretty house

   _____

2. a large and magnificent house

   _____

3. an old and famous movie

   _____

4. a large, pretty diamond

_____

5. a serious-minded, good student

_____

6. a kind and polite store clerk

_____

7. an old and valuable bonsai

_____

8. an unusual and beautiful flower

_____

9. a polite and refined person

_____

10. a young, energetic teacher

_____

11. easy and suitable textbook

_____

12. a modern and beautiful building

_____

13. a stupid and boring person

_____

14. a large, modern city

_____

15. a handsome and serious-minded doctor

_____

Using two adjectives (either **na** or _regular_) and an appropriate noun, describe the following things:

1. Times Square

_____

2. the Hope Diamond

_____

3. the Rock of Gibraltar

_____

4. Mr. Universe

_____

5. a favorite sweater you've had for five years

_____

6. a duchess

_____

7. a shady park

_____

8. leftover tempura from two weeks ago

_____

9. a duffer who curses when he misses his golf shot

_____

10. the nerd in your class who always gets an 'A'

_____

11. PERMISSION AND PROHIBITION
WITH NA ADJECTIVES

If you want to ask, for example, *Is it OK if it's quiet?* you would have to use the **-te** form of the **na** adjective and add one of the following endings, depending on how polite you want to sound:

. . . mo ii?	(plain)
. . . mo ii desu ka?	(formal)
. . . mo kamaimasen ka?	(super polite)
. . . wa dame desu ka?	(formal)
. . . wa ikemasen ka?	(super polite)

Note that the particle that precedes **dame** and **ikemasen** in this pattern is alwasys **wa.** While the **mo** particle in the patterns **mo ii, mo ii desu ka, mo kamaimasen ka** is often dropped in conversation, the particle **wa** with **dame** and **ikemasen** can never be dropped.

The above patterns are exactly those which we studied earlier in the section on *regular* adjectives. The only difference is that with **na** adjectives, you must use the **-te** form of **desu** or **ja arimasen** (for negatives).

Compare these sentences:

Shizuka de mo ii desu ka?	= Is it OK if it's quiet?
Shizuka ja nakute mo ii desu ka?	= Is it OK if it's not quiet?
Atsukute mo ii desu ka?	= Is it OK if it's hot?
Atsuku nakute mo ii desu ka?	= Is it OK if it's not hot?

If you want to give permission by saying, *it's OK if . . . , it doesn't matter if . . . , it's fine if . . . ,* you must use either:

. . . mo ii (desu).
. . . mo kamaimasen.

What do these sentences mean in English?

1. Koohii wa atsuku nakute mo ii desu ka?

2. Paatii wa nigiyaka ja nakute mo ii desu ka?

   _____

3. Uchi wa chotto fuben de mo ii?

   _____

4. Sensei wa yuumei ja nakute wa dame desu ka?

   _____

5. Heya wa kirei ja nakute mo kamaimasen.

   _____

6. Hon wa muzukashikute wa ikemasen ka?

   _____

7. Apaato wa anmari modan ja nakute mo ii desu.

   _____

8. Nihongo ga heta de mo kamaimasen ka?

   _____

9. Kooen wa tookute mo ii desu ka?

   _____

10. Toshokan wa shizuka ja nakute wa ikemasen ka?

    _____

The following sentences are examples of ways we ask or give permission in English. Write an equivalent Japanese sentence. Vary the level of speech for each sentence.

1. Is it OK if it's not safe?

   _____

2. Does it matter if it's slow?

   _____

3. Is it OK if the house isn't modern?

   _____

4. It's fine if the movie isn't famous.

   _____

5. It's OK if he doesn't play the piano well.

   _____

6. Is it OK if I don't play tennis well?

   _____

7. It's OK if the train isn't fast.

   _____

8. It's all right if the library isn't quiet.

   _____

9. It's OK if he isn't handsome.

   _____

10. Is it OK if the room isn't clean?

    _____

To say *something is not OK, wouldn't do,* or *it has to be,* etc. you need to use the following patterns:

> *-te* form + wa ikemasen > *shizuka de* wa ikemasen
> *-te* form + wa dame desu > *shizuka de* wa dame desu

Both these sentences mean *It won't do if it's quiet.*

Note that when you use the negative **-te** form with these patterns, you can think of the meaning in two ways:

> shizuka ja nakute wa ikemasen = It's not OK if it's not quiet.
> shizuka de nakute wa ikemasen = It has got to be quiet.

What do these sentences mean?

1. Toshokan wa shizuka ja nakute wa ikemasen.

   _____

2. Hoteru wa modan ja nakute wa ikemasen.

   _____

3. Biiru wa tsumetaku nakute wa ikemasen.

   _____

4. Gakusei wa majime ja nakute wa ikemasen.

   _____

5. Ten-in wa teinei ja nakute wa dame desu.

   _____

6. Kangofu wa shinsetsu de nakute wa ikemasen.

   _____

7. Isha wa baka de wa ikemasen.

   _____

8. Joyuu wa kirei ja nakute wa dame desu.

   _____

9. Uchi wa fuben de wa ikemasen.

   _____

10. Hikooki wa hayaku nakute wa dame desu.

    _____

Write an equivalent Japanese sentence for the following sentences. Don't be fooled by the English wording!

1. The school has to be safe.
   _____

2. It's not OK if the school is not safe.
   _____

3. The sushi has to be fresh.
   _____

4. It's not OK if the park is quiet.
   _____

5. It's not OK if the park is not quiet.
   _____

6. The park has to be quiet.
   _____

7. It won't do if the post office is inconvenient.
   _____

8. The post office has to be convenient.
   _____

The following questions will ask you permission. Answer using the cues of **hai, ee** (yes), or **iie** (no).

1. Apaato wa modan ja nakute mo ii desu ka?
   Iie. _____

2. Eiga wa yuumei ja nakute mo ii desu ka?
   Hai. _____

3. Resutoran wa shizuka ja nakute mo ii desu ka?
   Iie. _____

4. Hana wa shiroku nakute wa ikemasen ka?
   Ee. _____

5. Tekisuto wa kuwashiku nakute mo kamaimasen ka?
   Iie. _____

6. Zasshi wa furukute mo ii desu ka?
   Iie. _____

7. Heya wa kirei ja nakute mo ii desu ka?
   Hai. _____

8. Koora wa tsumetaku nakute mo ii desu ka?
   Hai. _____

12. "EVEN IF"

So far, you have seen one application of the **-te** form + **mo** in the permission pattern. In this chapter, the **-te** form + **mo** of both *regular* adjectives and **na** adjectives will be used in other ways to mean *even if.* If you wanted to say *Even if it's expensive, I'll buy it,* you would need to use **-te mo**.

Example: Takakute mo kaimasu. = Even if it's expensive, I'll buy it.

Write the equivalent for the following sentences:

1. **Furukute mo** kaimasu.

   _____

2. **Yasuku nakute mo** kaimasu.

   _____

3. Watashi wa **genki ja nakute mo** ikimasu.

   _____

4. **Hima de mo** ikimasen.

   _____

5. Sono hon wa **yuumei de mo** yomimasen.

   _____

6. Sono tekisuto wa **yokute mo** irimasen.

   _____

7. Sono kooen wa **abunakute mo** ikimasu.

   _____

8. Sono joyuu wa **kirei de mo** kirai desu.

   _____

9. Sono mise wa **fuben de mo** itsumo ikimasu.

   _____

10. **Heta de mo** nihongo de hanashimasu.

    _____

As you can see from the examples above, the clause after **-te mo** can end in a verb, an adjective, or noun **desu.**

Now, translate these sentences into Japanese:

1. Even if they're not pretty, I'll buy them.

   _____

2. Even if they're not fresh, I'll buy them.

   _____

3. Even if it's not comfortable, I'll buy it.

   _____

4. Even if it's not quiet, I'll go.

   _____

5. Even if the restaurant is not quiet, I'll go.

   _____

6. Even if it's dangerous, I'll go.

   _____

7. Even if she's not polite I'll ask.

   _____

8. Even if the store clerk is not polite, I'll ask.

   _____

9. Even if she's not kind, I'll ask.

   _____

10. Even if the nurse is not kind, I'll ask.

    _____

11. Even if it's no problem, I'll ask.

    _____

12. Even if the park is pretty, I won't go.

    _____

13. Even if my Japanese is bad, I'll speak it.

    _____

14. Even if the textbook is difficult, I'll read it.

    _____

15. Even if my head (doesn't hurt) isn't painful, I won't go.

    _____

13. THE -BA FORM OF NA ADJECTIVES

The conditional form of **na** adjectives is made by using the -**ba** form of **desu** which is **nara**. In formal written style, **naraba** is often used but in conversation, **nara** is considered a correct form and is more often heard than **naraba**.

The conditional phrase *If it's quiet* is: **shizuka nara**.

As you can see, this is a much easier construction than the -**ba** form of *regular* adjectives where -**kereba** is added to the adjective stem as in samu**kereba** (*if it's cold*).

In English, other expressions which would require use of the -**ba** form in Japanese would be *provided that . . .* and *as long as . . .*

In the following exercise, give the -**ba** form of the adjective indicated and write the meaning in English. Again, *regular* adjectives will be mixed in, so be on the alert!

1. benri > _____
    (Eng.) _____

2. joohin > _____
    _____

3. kitanai > _____
    _____

4. tooi > _____
    _____

5. suteki > _____
    _____

6. majime > _____
    _____

   7. taisetsu > _____

         _____

   8. yasui > _____

         _____

   9. rippa > _____

         _____

  10. raku > _____

         _____

The negative conditional of **na** adjectives is formed by adding **ja nakereba** to the **na** adjective as in:

shizuka ja nakereba = if it is not quiet

Contrast this form to the negative conditional of *regular* adjectives where **-ku nakereba** is added to the verb stem as in:

tanoshiku nakereba = if it is not fun

Change the following sentences into a negative conditional form. Be on the lookout for *regular* adjectives.

   1. Yoku arimasen. > _____

   2. Nigiyaka ja arimasen. > _____

   3. Taikutsu ja arimasen. > _____

   4. Ookiku arimasen. > _____

   5. Hansamu ja arimasen. > _____

   6. Atarashiku arimasen. > _____

   7. Genki ja arimasen. > _____

   8. Hima ja arimasen. > _____

9. Oishiku arimasen. > _____

10. Mazuku arimasen. > _____

11. Majime ja arimasen. > _____

12. Hen ja arimasen. > _____

In the next exercise, give a Japanese equivalent for each conditional clause. This is a mixed drill, with affirmatives and negatives of both *regular* adjectives and **na** adjectives.

1. If it's quiet

    _____

2. If it's *not* lively

    _____

3. If it's inconvenient

    _____

4. If it's dirty

    _____

5. If it's *not* clean

    _____

6. If you *don't* have free time

    _____

7. If it's *not* comfortable

    _____

8. If it's strange

    _____

9. If he's *not* famous

    _____

10. If it's *not* red

    _____

Usually, the subject of the *if* clause is marked with the particle **ga.** This rule is not etched in stone, so there might be times when you will see the subject marked by the particle **wa.** However, for our purposes here, let's get in the habit of using **ga** to indicate the subject of the *if* clause.

Other rules pertaining to the *if* clause which were mentioned in the section on *regular* adjectives can also be applied to **na** adjectives.

Figure out what the following sentences mean:

1. Sono kissaten ga shizuka nara, ikimasu.

2. Sono kutsu ga raku ja nakereba, kaimasen.

3. Sono sushi ga oishiku nakereba, tabemasen.

4. Ashita hima nara, ikimasu.

5. Ashita isogashikereba, ikimasen.

6. Genki nara, ikimasu.

7. Hana ga kirei nara, kaimasu.

8. Hana ga kirei ja nakereba, kaimasen.

9. Doresu ga joohin ja nakereba, irimasen.

10. Gakusei ga majime ja nakereba, dame desu.

Now you try making sentences ending with **yoku arimasen** (it's not good). Keep in mind that whatever the position of the *if* clause in English, the **-ba** clause can *never* end a sentence in Japanese.

1. If it's not clean, it's not good.

2. If the restaurant isn't quiet, it's not good.

3. If the school is inconvenient, it's not good.

4. It's not good if the class is boring.

5. It's not good if the students are not serious.

   _____

6. It's not good if the nurses aren't kind.

   _____

7. It's not good if the beer isn't cold.

   _____

8. It's not good if the teachers are not polite.

   _____

9. It's not good if the weather is bad.

   _____

10. It's not good if the park is dangerous.

    _____

Now, try combining *if* clauses with a verb in the second part of the sentence.

1. If the sweater is pretty, I'll buy it.

   _____

2. If it's a famous novel, I'll read it.

   _____

3. If they are modern paintings, I'll look at them.

   _____

4. If he's handsome, I'll meet him.

   _____

5. If I have free time, I'll go.

   _____

6. If I'm not well, I won't go.

   _____

7. If it's no good (broken), I won't buy it.

   _____

8. If the water is cold, I'll drink it.

   _____

9. If the shoes are cheap, I don't want them.

   _____

10. If the car is safe, I'll drive it.

    _____

14. "IT HAS TO BE . . ."

If you want to say *It has to be clean,* or *It must be clean,* you can use the following formula:

na [adj.] + [*negative* **-ba** *form*] + **narimasen**

Thus:

Kirei + ja nakereba + narimasen. = It has to be clean.

Notice the double negative in this construction which translates to an affirmative sentence.

Try these sentences yourself:

1. It has to be magnificent.

   _____

2. It has to be modern.

   _____

3. The students have to be serious.

   _____

4. Nurses have to be kind.

   _____

5. Store clerks have to be polite.

   _____

6. The station has to be convenient.

   _____

7. Schools must be safe.

   _____

8. Children must be healthy.

   _____

9. The shoes have to be chic.

   _____

10. The novel has to be famous.

    _____

The negative **-ba** form + **narimasen** was also studied in the section on *regular* adjectives. In the following mixed drill exercise, determine whether the adjective needed is a **na** adjective or *regular* adjective, then translate the sentence using the correct forms.

1. The car has to be red.

   _____

2. The doctors must be kind.

   _____

3. The hospital has to be near.

   _____

4. The store clerks have to be refined.

   _____

5. The store must be magnificent.

   _____

6. The building has to be modern.

   _____

7. The soup has to be hot.

   _____

8. The wine has to be chilled.

   _____

9. The department store has to be convenient.

   _____

10. The textbooks have to be appropriate.

    _____

11. The meat has to be fresh.

    _____

12. The train has to be fast.

    _____

13. The actors have to be handsome.

    _____

14. The rooms have to be clean.

    _____

15. The movie has to be interesting.

    _____

This pattern is equivalent in meaning to the negative **-te** form + **wa ikemasen.** That is,

      Kirei **ja nakereba narimasen.** = Kirei **ja nakute wa ikemasen.**

Both sentences mean *It must be clean,* or *It has to be clean.*

By the same token:

Atsuku nakereba narimasen. = Atsuku **nakute wa ikemasen.**

Both of the above sentences mean *It has to be hot,* or *It must be hot.*

Give the alternative form for the following:

1. Modan ja nakereba narimasen

   _____

2. Tsumetaku nakute wa ikemasen

   _____

3. Anzen ja nakereba narimasen

   _____

4. Genki ja nakute wa ikemasen

   _____

5. Yoku nakereba narimasen

   _____

6. Atarashiku nakute wa ikemasen

   _____

7. Yasuku nakute wa ikemasen

   _____

8. Majime ja nakute wa ikemasen

   _____

9. Yuumei ja nakereba narimasen

   _____

10. Benri ja nakute wa ikemasen

    _____

11. Omoshiroku nakereba narimasen

    _____

12. Shinsetsu ja nakereba narimasen

    _____

In Japanese, **na** [adj.] **ja nakereba narimasen ka?** can be used also to ask permission, meaning *Does it have to be . . . ?* Such a question can be answered in the same way you would answer any question asking permission.

Q: Kirei ja nakereba narimasen ka?
A (affirmative): Hai. Kirei ja nakereba narimasen. / Kirei ja nakute wa ikemasen.
A (negative): Iie. Kirei ja nakute mo ii desu. (No. It doesn't have to be pretty.)

In the following exercise, write an appropriate *permission* question using the above pattern.

1. _____
   Iie. Kirei ja nakute mo ii desu.

2. _____
   Hai. Joohin ja nakereba narimasen.

3. _____
   Iie. Atarashiku nakute mo ii desu.

4. _____
   Hai. Benri ja nakereba narimasen.

5. _____
   Iie. Ookiku nakute mo ii desu.

6. _____
   Hai. Modan ja nakereba narimasen.

7. _____
   Iie. Yasuku nakute mo ii desu.

8. _____
   Hai. Majime ja nakereba narimasen.

9. _____
   Iie. Shinsetsu ja nakute mo ii desu.

10. _____
    Hai. Suteki ja nakereba narimasen.

15. Soo Desu with na Adjectives

In the section on *regular* adjectives, we studied the construction **soo desu** to report hearsay (*I understand that . . .* , *I hear that . . .*). To say the sentence *I understand that she is pretty,* using the **na** adjective **kirei**, you would add **soo desu** to the plain form of the sentence **kirei desu**.

Example: Kirei **da** soo desu. = I hear that she is pretty.

Here are other possibilities using a **na** adjective and **soo desu**:

Kirei **ja nai** soo desu.   = I understand she *is not* pretty.
Kirei **datta** soo desu.   = I hear it *was* pretty.
Kirei **ja nakatta** soo desu.= I hear they *weren't* pretty.

Translate these sentences into Japanese:

1. I hear that he was rude.

2. I understand that she wasn't well.

3. I hear that it wasn't inconvenient.

4. I hear that she was kind.

5. I hear that they weren't comfortable.

6. I understand that it's chic.

7. I understand that it's not modern.

8. I hear that he's handsome.

9. I hear that it's not clean.

10. I hear that it wasn't suitable.

11. I understand that it was magnificent.

12. I understand that he isn't stupid.

13. I hear that they're no good.

14. I hear that he has free time.

15. I understand that he was famous.

16. I understand that he wasn't polite.

17. I hear that it's convenient.

18. I understand that they're not serious.

19. I hear that it was boring.

20. I understand that she's not stupid.

What do these sentences mean in English?

1. Ano daigaku no gakusei wa majime da soo desu.

2. Ano eiga wa zenzen taikutsu ja nakatta soo desu.

3. Ano eiga haiyuu wa totemo hansamu datta soo desu.

4. Eki no toire wa anmari kirei ja nai soo desu.

5. Tanaka-san no akachan wa totemo genki da soo desu.

6. Byooki wa moo daijoobu da soo desu.

7. Ano hito no kotoba wa anmari teinei ja nakatta soo desu.

8. Kono byooin no kangofu wa totemo shinsetsu da soo desu.

9. Nihongo no tekisuto wa anmari tekitoo ja nakatta soo desu.

10. Kimono wa anmari raku ja nai soo desu.

Now try expressing these ideas in Japanese. Use the above examples for help in constructing your sentences.

1. I understand that this department store's shoes aren't comfortable.

2. I understand that his language is very polite.

3. I hear that the doctors at that hospital aren't kind.

4. I understand that the hospital is very modern.

5. I hear that the university cafeteria is not very clean.

6. I hear that the class was very boring.

7. I hear that the weather in summer is always strange.

8. I understand that the school telephones are no good.

9. I hear that his German was very proficient.

10. I understand that he doesn't like Japanese food.

11. I hear that he doesn't have a lot of free time.

12. I hear that Tokyo is very lively at night.

Keep in mind that **soo desu** can be used after any plain form.

Example: Kirei ja nakute mo ii soo desu. =
I understand that it doesn't have to be clean.

Here, **soo desu** follows the plain form of the adjective **ii desu** used in the permission pattern.

Example: Kirei ja nakute wa ikenai soo desu. =
I understand that it has to be clean.

In this case, **ikenai** is the plain form of the verb **ikemasen.**

Example: Kirei ja nakereba **naranai** soo desu. =
I understand that it must be clean.

In the above example, **naranai** is the plain form of the verb **narimasen.**

Further, compare these two sentences:

Kooen wa anmari **kirei ja nai** soo desu. =
I understand that the park is not very clean.

Anmari **kirei na** kooen ja nai soo desu. =
I understand that it's not a very clean park.

In the first case, the **na** adjective appears in the predicate, while in the second the adjective modifies the noun **kooen.**

Using the above examples, figure out what is being said in the following sentences.

1. Kutsu wa raku ja nakute wa ikenai soo desu.
   _____

2. Sensei wa kibishku nakereba naranai soo desu.
   _____

3. Anmari shinsetsu na hito ja nai soo desu.
   _____

4. Shizuka na resutoran ja nakute mo ii soo desu.
   _____

5. Iro wa kirei ja nakereba naranai soo desu.
   _____

6. Uchi wa modan ja nakute mo ii soo desu.
   _____

7. Yuumei na daigaku ja nakute mo ii soo desu.
   _____

Using the above examples as a guide, try translating the following sentences. Some sentences will require you to use **na** adjectives. For others, you will need to use *regular* adjectives.

1. I understand that the schools have to be convenient.

    _____

2. I understand that he is a handsome teacher.

    _____

3. I hear that the sweater has to be black.

    _____

4. I understand that it's OK if the restaurant is quiet.

    _____

5. I hear that the room has to be clean.

    _____

6. I hear that the test doesn't have to be difficult.

    _____

7. I understand that she isn't a kind person.

    _____

8. I understand that your English has to be proficient.

    _____

9. I hear that he likes Japanese food.

    _____

10. I understand that spring is warm.

    _____

16. -SOO NOT SOO

In Japanese, **-soo** may be added to any **na** adjective to express the idea that something or someone looks, appears, or seems to be some way. This form allows you to make an assumption about a person or situation based on visual evaluation. Thus, someone who looks *refined* is **joohinsoo**. Whether the person is in fact refined is beside the point. In this respect, it differs from **deshoo**, as it does not address the question of probability.

As **-soo** is not a sentence-ending form, you can add **desu** or one of its forms to make a complete sentence.

Example: Ano kooen wa shizukasoo desu. = That park seems quiet.

Remember that this **-soo** differs from the **soo** studied earlier. Compare the meanings of the following sentences:

Joohin**soo** desu.   = She looks refined.
Joohin da **soo** desu. = I hear that she is refined.

Adjectives such as **kirei** and **hansamu** are never combined with this **-soo** when describing people, although **kireisoo** can be used to describe other situations or objects.

Using the **-soo** form, describe the following situations. Write in complete sentences:

1. You hear loud music, raucous laughter and voices coming from a restaurant. What would you say about the restaurant?

    _____

2. What observation would you make about a student wearing thick glasses and a pocket protector, carrying heavy tomes from the library?

    _____

3. You pass by a classroom where most of the students are either yawning or slumped over their desks. How do you think the lecture is?

    _____

4. You see a woman helping a handicapped person across the street. Describe the good samaritan.

    _____

5. You see an octogenarian running across the finish line at the Boston Marathon. Describe the old man.

6. A gossipy woman is on the phone all day spreading the news. How would you characterize her lifestyle?

7. An old man religiously tends to his bonsai tree. How would you characterize his feelings about the tree?

8. You see a woman immaculately dressed wearing a hat and white gloves, sipping tea with her pinky in the air. How does she look to you?

Compare the **-soo** form for *regular* adjectives and for **na** adjectives:

> muzukashii > muzukashi > muzukashisoo
> shizuka > shizukasoo

Remember that the *regular* adjective **ii** is irregular in this form (**yosasoo**).

Do the following exercise using the correct **-soo** form.

1. The teachers seem kind.

2. This street looks dangerous.

3. The test looks easy.

4. The students seem serious.

5. The baby looks very healthy.

6. This suit looks expensive.

7. This problem looks difficult.

8. The restaurant looks lively.

9. The library looks quiet.

10. The sweater looks very comfortable.

_____

11. These stores seem convenient.

_____

12. That man looks strong.

_____

13. She has time on her hands, doesn't she?

_____

14. The students look bored.

_____

15. That school looks good.

_____

The **-soo** form can also be used to modify nouns. Look at the following examples:

| himasoo na hito | = | a person who looks like he/she has free time |
| muzukashisoo na shiken | = | a difficult-looking test |

The above two phrases demonstrate that when describing a noun, the **-soo** form requires the use of the particle **na** before the noun. In other words, by adding **-soo** to either a *regular* adjective or a **na** adjective, you have created a new word which is treated like a **na** adjective.

Translate these phrases:

1. a healthy-looking baby

_____

2. a delicious-looking cake

_____

3. a diligent-looking child

_____

4. a sweater that looks warm

_____

5. a person who looks like he/she has spare time

_____

6. a cold-looking person

_____

7. comfortable-looking shoes

_____

8. a refined-looking woman

_____

9. a handy-looking dictionary

_____

10. a difficult-looking problem

_____

11. a coffee shop that looks quiet

_____

12. a kind-looking nurse

_____

13. a strict-looking teacher

_____

14. fresh-looking veggies

_____

15. a fun-looking party

_____

The **-soo** form can also describe a _verb_. When it does, the particle that follows it is **ni**.

You have already studied one way of expressing the idea _It looks hot_ using **desu** (which is not a verb). Let's learn another way of saying the same thing using a _verb_.

    Example: Ano hito no koohi wa atsusoo **ni** miemasu.

The verb **miemasu** means _something is visible,_ or _something can be seen._ The whole sentence would then mean _It (she,_ etc.) _is visible in a hot way_ or, in more idiomatic English, _It looks hot._

Patterning your sentences on the example above, translate these sentences. Remember to use the particle **ni** after the **-soo** form.

1. That person looks as if he's cold.

_____

2. The teacher looks kind.

_____

3. My friend looks lonely.

_____

4. That sweater looks warm.

_____

5. He looks like he's busy.

   _____

6. She looks like she has free time.

   _____

7. The building looks quiet.

   _____

8. The meat looks fresh.

   _____

9. This dress looks expensive.

   _____

10. She looks young.

    _____

11. The shoes look comfortable.

    _____

12. The students look diligent.

    _____

17. The -tari Form with na Adjectives

As with *regular* adjectives, the **-tari** form can be used with **na** adjectives to describe alternating or contrasting conditions such as *Sometimes it's clean and sometimes it's not.*

The affirmative and negative **-tari** forms are as follows:

> **na** adj. + dattari shimasu (desu)
> **na** adj. + ja nakattari shimasu (desu)

As with *regular* adjectives, the tense of the sentence is determined by the tense of **shimasu** or **desu**. **Shimasu** seems to be the more popular choice of the two.

A situation that flip-flops back and forth between two opposing states can be expressed in the following way:

> Kirei dattari kirei ja nakattari shimasu. =
> Sometimes it's clean and sometimes it's not.

Do the following exercise using the affirmative and negative **-tari** forms. The subject of the sentence can be marked by either **wa** or **ga**. Do not translate personal pronouns such as *you, he, she,* etc.

1. Sometimes the baby is healthy and sometimes he's not.

   _____

2. Sometimes they're comfortable and sometimes they're not.

   _____

3. Sometimes the doctors are kind and sometimes they're not.

   _____

4. Sometimes he's polite and sometimes he's not.

   _____

5. Sometimes I have free time and sometimes I don't.

   _____

6. Sometimes the class is boring and sometimes it's not.

   _____

7. Sometimes the students are diligent and sometimes they're not.

   _____

8. Sometimes novels are famous and sometimes they're not.

Na adjectives can be combined with *regular* adjectives in one sentence.

Example: Isogashikattari hima dattari shimasu. =
           Sometimes I'm busy and sometimes I have free time.

Do the following exercise using the correct form of the adjective (*regular* or **na**):

1. Sometimes they're polite and sometimes they're rude.

---

2. Sometimes the restaurant is quiet and sometimes it's lively.

---

3. Sometimes the class is boring and sometimes it's fun.

---

4. Sometimes the sushi is good (tasting) and sometimes it's awful
    (tasting).

---

5. Sometimes the towns are modern and sometimes they're old.

---

6. Sometimes the students are proficient in English and sometimes
    they're not good at it.

---

7. Sometimes the fruit is OK and sometimes it's no good.

---

8. Sometimes we're busy and sometimes we have free time.

---

9. Sometimes it's clean and sometimes it's dirty.

---

10. Sometimes it's noisy and sometimes it's quiet.

Answer these questions in Japanese using the **-tari** form:

1. Mainichi tenki ga ii desu ka?

---

2. Anata wa mainichi isogashii deshoo?

---

3. Kono mise no yasai wa doo desu ka?

   _____

4. Nihongo no kurasu wa omoshiroi desu ka?

   _____

5. Daigaku no kafeteria wa itsumo nigiyaka desu ka?

   _____

6. Anata no heya wa kirei desu ka?

   _____

7. Nihongo no sensei wa shinsetsu desu ka?

   _____

8. Amerika no gakusei wa Nihongo ga joozu desu ka?

   _____

18. THE NA ADJECTIVE AND SUGIMASU

Na adjectives as well as *regular* adjectives may be combined with -sugimasu to mean that something is *too . . .* or *excessively . . .*

The **na** adjective can be added as is to the verb **sugimasu** in this construction. Thus, the sentence *It is too modern* is:

Modansugimasu.

The subject of the predicate is marked by either the particle **wa** or **ga**.

Do the following exercise using the appropriate **na** adjective and -sugimasu. Remember that the past tense of **sugimasu** is **sugimashita**.

1. The restaurant is too quiet.

   _____

2. I have too much free time.

   _____

3. Department store clerks are too polite.

   _____

4. These buildings are too modern.

   _____

5. This party is too loud (lively).

   _____

6. This music is too famous.

   _____

Review this construction using *regular* adjectives and do the following exercise using the appropriate *regular* or **na** adjective:

1. The test was too hard.

   _____

2. The movie was too boring.

   _____

3. I had too much free time on my hands.

   _____

4. This road is too dangerous.

   _____

5. That car is too expensive.

   _____

6. He is too diligent.

   _____

7. That house is too inconvenient.

   _____

8. Tokyo is too bustling.

   _____

19. To Omoimasu

As we studied in the previous section on *regular* adjectives, expressions such as
. . . to omoimasu, and **. . . to iimashita** may follow plain forms. This is also true of
na adjectives.

To summarize, the plain forms of a **na** adjective are:

shizuka da.	=	It is quiet.
shizuka ja nai.	=	It is not quiet.
shizuka datta.	=	It was quiet.
shizuka ja nakatta.	=	It wasn't quiet.

Thus:

shizuka da **to omoimasu.**	=	I think it's quiet.
shizuka ja nakatta **to iimashita.**	=	He said it wasn't quiet.

Other expressions using the plain forms in this way are:

. . . to kikimashita	=	I heard that . . .
. . . to itte imasu	=	(Someone) is saying that . . .
. . . to kotaemashita	=	(Someone) answered that . . .

If mentioned, the subject of both the adjective and verb can be marked by either the
particles **wa** or **ga**. For example:

Sono **resutoran wa** shizuka da to **tomodachi ga** iimashita. =
My friend said that the restaurant is quiet.

Write the English equivalent of the following sentences:

1. Kyooto wa kirei da to kikimashita.

2. Kono daigaku no gakusei wa majime ja nai to sensei ga itte imasu.

3. Sono tekisuto wa tekitoo ja nai to sensei ga iimashita.

4. Ano hito wa yuumei datta to kotaemashita.

   _____

5. Tomu Kuruuzu wa hansamu da to omoimasu.

   _____

6. Kono kooen wa anzen ja nai to kikimashita.

   _____

7. Sono koosu wa totemo taikutsu datta to tomodachi ga itte imasu.

   _____

8. Sono byooin no kangofu wa anmari shinsetsu ja nakatta to kikimashita.

   _____

Now translate these sentences. **Na** adjectives are mixed in with _regular_ adjectives.

1. I heard that this department store's clerks are not polite.

   _____

2. My friend answered that he doesn't have free time.

   _____

3. I heard that the station is convenient.

   _____

4. I think that that team isn't strong.

   _____

5. I heard that the station is modern and convenient.

   _____

6. That person answered that he is very poor.

   _____

7. My friend said that Tokyo summers are hot.

   _____

8. I heard that the station is very near.

   _____

9. I think that New York's weather is strange.

   _____

10. I think that kimonos are not comfortable.

    _____

11. I heard that the university cafeteria was dirty.

    _____

12. My mother said that the doctors of that hospital are very kind.

    _____

13. She answered that she was OK.

    _____

14. Father says that this bonsai is very precious.

    _____

15. I heard that Ryooanji's garden is beautiful.

    _____

16. I think that these shoes aren't comfortable.

    _____

17. Father says that the bus isn't fast.

    _____

18. I heard that the facilities aren't new.

    _____

20. OOKII AND CHIISAI

As you learned in the previous section, **ookii** and **chiisai** are *regular* adjectives. However, when they *precede a noun,* they can also be treated as **na** adjectives:

$$\text{ooki na} \quad = \quad \text{ookii}$$
$$\text{chiisa na} \quad = \quad \text{chiisai}$$

These forms can be used interchangeably. The decision to use one form rather than the other seems to be a question of speaking style rather than of substance. Thus:

$$\text{ooki na uchi} \quad = \quad \text{ookii uchi}$$
$$\text{chiisa na kooen} \quad = \quad \text{chiisai kooen}$$

The **na** adjective form cannot be used when these adjectives appear in the predicate. Thus, "ooki desu" is not correct Japanese, nor is "ooki ja arimasen." When the adjective is in the predicate, it must be inflected.

Where appropriate, use the **na** adjective alternative in the following sentences:

1. It is a big sweater.

2. That sweater is not big.

3. That sweater was big.

4. It was a big sweater.

5. That sweater wasn't big.

6. I saw a small dog.

7. Small dogs are cute.

8. My dog isn't small.

9. It's a small town.

   _____

10. Fuji-san is a large mountain.

   _____

11. Mr. Tanaka is a large person.

   _____

12. It's not a big problem.

   _____

21. HOO GA II WITH NA ADJECTIVES

As you studied in the section on *regular* adjectives, **. . . hoo ga ii (desu)** is used when you want to say *something is better if . . .* This pattern can also be used with **na** adjectives.

Look at the following examples:

Resutoran wa shizuka na hoo ga ii desu. =
Restaurants are better if they're quiet.

Resutoran wa shizuka ja nai hoo ga ii desu. =
Restaurants are better if they're not quiet.

Note that in the affirmative, the **na** adjective is followed by the particle **na**, as the word **hoo** is a noun. In the negative, the plain form of **ja arimasen** is used. **Ja** may be replaced by the more formal **dewa**.

Review this pattern and its use with *regular* adjectives, then do the following exercise. You must first determine whether the adjective called for is a *regular* or **na** adjective.

1. Parks are better if they are lively.
   _____

2. It's better if the buildings are modern.
   _____

3. Art museums are better if they are old.
   _____

4. Fish are better if they are fresh.
   _____

5. It's better if the students are not too diligent.
   _____

6. It's better if the worker does not have a lot of free time.
   _____

7. It's better if the teachers are strict.
   _____

8. It's better if the rooms are clean.
   _____

9. Small hospitals are better.

   _____

10. It's better if the nurses are kind.

    _____

11. Salad is better if it's cold.

    _____

12. It's better if the painting is famous.

    _____

A few variations of **. . . hoo ga** . . . were mentioned earlier. Now that you have been working with **na** adjectives, you can study a few more.

    . . . no hoo ga raku desu = It's more comfortable if . . .
    . . . no hoo ga kirei desu = It's prettier (nicer looking) if . . .
    . . . no hoo ga benri desu = It's more convenient if . . .

Translate these sentences into English:

1. Hito ga ooi hoo ga anzen desu.

   _____

2. Seetaa wa ookii hoo ga raku desu.

   _____

3. Hana wa ookii hoo ga kirei desu.

   _____

4. Paatii wa nigiyaka na hoo ga omoshiroi desu.

   _____

5. Uchi wa chikai hoo ga benri desu.

   _____

6. Doresu wa akai hoo ga suteki desu.

   _____

7. Gakusei wa sukunai hoo ga omoshiroi desu.

   _____

8. Apaato wa modan na hoo ga suki desu.

   _____

9. Setsubi wa atarashii hoo ga benri desu.

   _____

10. Resutoran wa shizuka na hoo ga suki desu.

    _____

Using the above sentences as a guide, express the following sentences in Japanese:

1. It's more convenient if the station is nearby.

   _____

2. Big shoes are more comfortable.

   _____

3. Small dogs are cuter.

   _____

4. Modern buildings are nicer looking.

   _____

5. Old houses are more interesting.

   _____

6. Red sweaters are more chic.

   _____

7. I prefer lively parties.

   _____

8. New facilities are more convenient.

   _____

9. Parks are safer if there are a lot of people.

   _____

10. Old towns are more famous.

    _____

22. THE PRETTIER THE BETTER

In the section on *regular* adjectives (p. 83), you learned how to say such sentences as *As for coffee, the hotter it is, the better.* This construction is also applicable to **na** adjectives. Look at the following sentence and compare it to the construction for *regular* adjectives:

> Kirei nara kirei na hodo ii desu. = The prettier (it is) the better.

The fact that the **na** adjective is not inflected makes this pattern easy to form as compared to *regular* adjectives. The only factor you must keep in mind is the use of **na** before **hoo** which does not occur with *regular* adjectives.

Adjectives other than **ii** may be used to end the sentence. **Omoshiroi, oishii, suki,** and **raku** are just a few examples of the versatility of this pattern. Although not studied here, such **hodo** sentences may also be combined with verbs.

> Example: Okane wa ookereba ooi hodo raku desu. =
> The more money, the easier it is.

What do the following sentences mean? Both *regular* adjectives and **na** adjectives are used.

1. Hana wa ookereba ooi hodo kirei desu.

   _____

2. Sensei wa majime nara majime na hodo ii desu.

   _____

3. Paatii wa nigiyaka nara nigiykaka na hodo omoshiroi.

   _____

4. Mise wa chikakereba chikai hodo benri desu.

   _____

5. Machi wa modan nara modan na hodo kirei desu.

   _____

6. Haiyuu wa hansamu nara hansamu na hodo ii desu.

   _____

7. Nihongo ga joozu nara joozu na hodo ii desu.

   _____

8. Kutsu wa furukereba furui hodo raku desu.

   _____

9. Setsubi wa atarashikereba atarashii hodo benri desu.

   _____

10. Wain wa furukereba furui hodo takai desu.

    _____

11. Kuruma wa ookikereba ookii hodo anzen desu.

    _____

12. Me ga ookikereba ookii hodo kawaii desu.

    _____

Using **na** adjectives indicated, practice making the first part of this construction.

Example: genki > genki nara genki na hodo

1. clean >

   _____

2. famous >

   _____

3. modern >

   _____

4. convenient >

   _____

5. having free time >

   _____

6. diligent >

   _____

7. attractive >

   _____

8. polite >

   _____

9. safe >

   _____

10. magnificent >

    _____

Express the following sentences in Japanese. Don't be misled by the variations in the English sentences. They will follow the pattern of the preceding two exercises. You will have to use *regular* adjectives and **na** adjectives in this exercise.

1. The more attractive, the better.

2. As for wines, the older they are, the more expensive.

3. The safer schools are, the better.

4. The more convenient the house is, the better.

5. The larger the house, the more expensive.

6. The more modern the painting, the more interesting.

7. The more free time I have, the more bored I am.

8. The fresher the meat, the more delicious it is.

9. As for bonsai, the smaller they are, the more interesting they are.

10. The larger the dog, the cuter it is.

11. As for buildings, the more modern they are, the cleaner they are.

12. The further away the stores are, the more inconvenient they are.

13. As for dresses, the more chic they are, they more expensive they are.

14. The quieter the park, the more I like it.

15. The older the movie, the more interesting it is.

GLOSSARY OF NOUNS (JAPANESE – ENGLISH)

A

akachan	baby
Amerika	the U.S., America
Amerikajin	American person
apaato	apartment
ashita	tomorrow
atama	head (part of body)

B

bangumi	TV program
basu	bus
biiru	beer
bijutsukan	museum
biru	building
bonsai	bonsai (miniature tree)
byooin	hospital

C

chichi	father (one's own)
chiimu	team

D

daigaku	college, university
daiya	diamond
deeto	date (with a friend)
densha	train
denwa	telephone
depaato	department store
doitsugo	the German language
dooshite	why
doresu	dress
doyoobi	Saturday

E

e	painting
eiga	movie
eigo	the English language
eki	station

F

furuutsu	fruit
fuyu	winter

G

gakkoo	school
gakusei	student
geemu	game
gohan	rice (cooked), meal
gorufu	golf

H

haha	mother (one's own)
haiyuu	actor
hana	flower
haru	spring
heya	room
hi	day
hikooki	airplane
hito	person, people
Hokkaidoo	Hokkaido
hon	book
hoteru	hotel

I

ima	now
inu	dog
isha	doctor (physician)
iwa	rock

J

jisho	dictionary
joyuu	actress
juusu	juice

K

kabe	wall
kafeteria	cafeteria
kangofu	nurse

karaa terebi	color TV
karee raisu	curry rice
keeki	cake
keshiki	view
kimochi	feeling
kinoo	yesterday
kippu	ticket
kissaten	coffee shop
kodomo	child, children
koko	here
konpyuuta	computer
koocha	English (black) tea
kooen	park
koohii	coffee
koora	cola, Coke
koosu	(school, college) course
kooto	coat
kotoba	language
kuchi	mouth
kudamono	fruit
kuni	country (nation, region)
kurasu	class (school)
kuruma	car
kusuri	medicine, medication
kutsu	shoes
kyonen	last year
kyoo	today
Kyooto	Kyoto (city)

M

machi	city, town
mainichi	everyday
me	eye
michi	road, street
mise	store, shop
mizu	water
mondai	problem

N

natsu	summer
neko	cat
Nihon	Japan
Nihongo	the Japanese language
Nihonjin	Japanese person
niku	meat
niwa	garden, yard
nomimono	drink

O

ocha	(Japanese) tea
okaasan	mother (honorific)
okashi	sweets
ongaku	music
onna no hito	woman (polite)
onna no ko	girl
otoko	man
otoko no hito	man (polite)
otoko no ko	boy
otoosan	father (honorific)

P

paatii	party
pan	bread
piano	piano
piza	pizza

R

rajio	radio
resutoran	restaurant
ryoori	cooking

S

sakana	fish
sake	rice wine
sarada	salad
sashimi	raw fish
se	height, physical stature
seetaa	sweater
sensei	teacher
senshuu	last week
setsubi	facilities
setsumei	explanation
shatsu	tee shirt, polo shirt
shinkansen	the bullet train
shigoto	work
shiitsu	sheets
shinbun	newspaper
shoosetsu	novel
sokkusu	socks
sooji	housecleaning
sora	sky
sukaato	skirt
supeingo	the Spanish language
suupu	soup
suutsu	suit

T

tabemono	food
tekisuto	textbook
ten-in	store clerk
tenisu	tennis
tenki	weather
terebi	TV
toire	bathroom
tokei	watch, clock
tokoro	place
tomodachi	friend
Tookyoo	Tokyo
toshokan	library

U

uchi	house, home

W

wain	wine
wanpiisu	dress (one piece)
watashi	I

Y

yama	mountain
yasai	vegetable
yuubinkyoku	post office

Z

zasshi	magazine

GLOSSARY OF NOUNS (ENGLISH – JAPANESE)

Plurals are not listed, as all nouns in Japanese can be singular and plural at the same time.

A

actor	haiyuu
actress	joyuu
American (person)	Amerikajin
apartment building	apaato
art museum	bijutsukan

B

baby	akachan
bathroom	toire
beer	biiru
book	hon
boy	otoko no ko
bread	pan
building	biru
bullet train	shinkansen
bus	basu

C

cafeteria	kafeteria
cake	keeki
car	kuruma
cat	neko
child	kodomo
class	kurasu
clock	tokei
coffee	koohii
coffee shop	kissaten
coat	kooto
cola, Coke	koora
college (in school)	daigaku
color TV	karaa terebi
computer	konpyuuta
cooking	ryoori
country	kuni
course	koosu
curry rice	karee raisu

D

date (with a person)	deeto
day	hi
department store	depaato
diamond	daiyaa
dictionary	jisho
doctor	isha
dog	inu
dress	doresu, wanpiisu
drink	nomimono

E

ear	mimi
English (language)	eigo
everyday	mainichi
explanation	setsumei
eye	me

F

facilities	setsubi
father	chichi (your own), otoosan
feeling	kimochi
flower	hana
fish	sakana
food	tabemono
friend	tomodachi
fruit	kudamono, furuutsu

G

game	geemu
garden	niwa
German (language)	doitsugo
girl	onna no ko
golf	gorufu

H

head	atama
height	se
here	koko
Hokkaido	Hokkaidoo (northern most island)
home	uchi
hospital	byooin
hotel	hoteru
housecleaning	sooji

J

Japan	Nihon
Japanese language	Nihongo
Japanese person	Nihonjin
juice	juusu

K

Kyoto	Kyooto (city)

L

language	kotoba
library	toshokan

M

magazine	zasshi
man	otoko (no hito)
meat	niku
medicine	kusuri
mother	haha (your own), okaasan
mountain	yama
mouth	kuchi
movie	eiga
music	ongaku

N

newspaper	shinbun
novel	shoosetsu
now	ima
nurse	kangofu

P

painting	e
park	kooen

party   paatii

party	paatii
person	hito
piano	piano
pizza	piza
place	tokoro
plane	hikooki
post office	yuubinkyoku
problem	mondai
program	bangumi

R

radio	rajio
raw fish	sashimi
restaurant	resutoran
rice	gohan
rice wine	sake
road	michi
rock	iwa
room	heya

S

salad	sarada
Saturday	Doyoobi
school	gakkoo
sheet	shiitsu
shirt	shatsu
skirt	sukaato
shoes	kutsu
sky	sora
socks	sokkusu
soup	suupu
Spanish language	Supeingo
spring	haru
station	eki
store	mise
store clerk	ten-in
student	gakusei
suit	suutsu
summer	natsu
sweater	seetaa
sweets	okashi

T

tea	koocha (English), o-cha (Japanese)
teacher	sensei
team	chiimu
telephone	denwa

tennis	tenisu
textbook	tekisuto
ticket	kippu
today	kyoo
tomorrow	ashita
town	machi
train	densha
Tokyo	Tookyoo

U

United States	Amerika
university	daigaku

V

vegetable	yasai
view	keshiki

W

wall	kabe
watch	tokei
water	mizu
weather	tenki
why	dooshite
wine	wain
winter	fuyu
woman	onna no hito
word	kotoba
work	shigoto

Y

yesterday	kinoo

ANSWER KEY

Page 14

1. atsui 2. atsui 3. atarashii 4. osoi 5. ookii
6. warui 7. takai 8. chikai 9. samui / tsumetai
10. hayai 11. muzukashii 12. oishii 13. yasui
14. chiisai 15. furui 16. ii 17. tooi 18. yasashii
19. mazui 20. karai

1. takai 2. tooi 3. isogashii

Page 15

4. muzukashii / yasashii 5. oishii 6. ii
7. tanoshii 8. ookii 9. furui 10. karai
11. hayai 12. chiisai

Page 16

1. furui 2. takai 3. ookii

1. yasui kuruma
2. atarashii terebi
3. omoshiroi eiga
4. atsui koohii
5. tsumetai nomimono
6. atatakai hi
7. atarashii yasai

Page 17

8. furui rajio
9. isogashii hi
10. tsumetai hito
11. ookii inu
12. chiisai neko
13. tooi tokoro
14. takai seetaa
15. ii hon

1. Omoshiroi eiga deshita.
2. Oishii sushi ja arimasen.
3. Atsui koohii deshita.
4. Ii hon desu ka?
5. Atarashii terebi ja arimasen deshita.
6. Ii gakkoo deshita.

Page 18

7. Chikai resutoran desu.

8. Ookii neko ja arimasen deshita.
9. Chiisai inu ja arimasen.
10. Muzukashii mondai deshita.
11. Ookii yuubinkyoku ja arimasen
12. Takai depaato ja arimasen.

Page 19

1. Sono rajoi wa ii desu.
2. Ano biiru wa oishii desu.
3. Gakkoo wa chikai desu.
4. Kyoo wa isogashii desu.
5. Kono terebi wa ookii desu.
6. Ano sakana wa furui desu.
7. Ano sushi wa mazui desu.
8. Hikooki wa hayai desu.
9. Tempura wa yasui desu.
10. Sensei wa yasashii desu.

Page 20

1. Atsui desu.
2. Isogashii desu.
3. Muzukashii desu.
4. Suzushii desu.
5. Nihongo wa yasashii desu.

1. Atatakai.
2. Koohii wa atsui.
3. Kuruma wa atarashii.
4. Resutoran wa takai.
5. Yasai wa atarashii.

1. tooi 2. chiisai 3. ookii 4. yasashii
5. takai 6. muzukashii 7. yasui 8. tanoshii
9. atsui 10. isogashii 11. chiisai 12. furui
13. atatakai 14. atsui 15. atarashii 16. ii
17. karai 18. hayai 19. mazui 20. oishii

Page 21

1. atarashiku arimasen
2. yoku arimasen
3. isogashiku arimasen
4. furuku arimasen
5. hayaku arimasen
6. amaku arimasen

7. tanoshiku arimasen
8. omoshiroku arimasen
9. takaku arimasen
10. yasuku arimasen
11. muzukashiku arimasen
12. ookiku arimasen

Page 22
13. tooku arimasen
14. waruku arimasen
15. mazuku arimasen

1. Iie. Ookiku arimasen.
2. Iie. Chikaku arimasen.
3. Iie. Omoshiroku arimasen.
4. Iie. Muzukashiku arimasen.
5. Iie. Atarashiku arimasen.
6. Iie. Yoku arimasen.
7. Iie. Mazuku arimasen
8. Iie. Atsuku arimasen.
9. Iie. Tsumetaku arimasen.
10. Iie. Karaku arimasen.

Page 23
1. Atsuku arimasen.
2. Isogashiku arimasen.
3. Sono koohii wa tsumetaku arimasen.
4. Sono kuruma wa atarashiku arimasen.
5. Sono juusu wa amaku arimasen.
6. Sono tempura wa oishiku arimasen.
7. Sono zasshi wa yoku arimasen.
8. Sono yasai wa atarashiku arimasen.
9. Sono mondai wa muzukashiku arimasen.
10. Sono gakkoo wa tooku arimasen.
11. Sono inu wa ookiku arimasen.
12. Sono eiga wa omoshiroku arimasen.

Page 24
1. Omoshiroku nai. It is not interesting.
2. Kore wa atarashiku nai. This is not new (fresh).
3. Kono zasshi wa waruku nai. This magazine is not bad.
4. Kono koohii wa atsuku nai. This coffee isn't hot.
5. Ano kuruma wa furuku nai. That car isn't old.

1. Ano neko wa ookiku nai.
2. Shiken wa muzukashiku nai.

3. Uchi wa chiisaku nai.
4. Kyoo wa suzushiku nai.
5. Kono seetaa wa atatakaku nai.
6. Fuyu wa samuku nai.
7. Piza wa mazuku nai.
8. Ano hon wa yoku nai.
9. Nihon wa tooku nai.
10. Kyoo wa tanoshiku nai.

Page 25
1. Sono suupu wa atsuku nai.
2. Sono uchi wa ookiku nai.
3. Kyoo wa atsuku nai.
4. Sono zasshi wa omoshiroku nai.
5. Sono setsumei wa muzukashiku nai.
6. Sono sensei wa yasashiku nai.
7. Sono jisho wa yoku nai.
8. Kyoo wa atatakaku nai.
9. Sono terebi wa atarashiku nai.
10. Sono eki wa tooku nai.
11. Nihon wa chikaku nai.
12. Sono kippu wa takaku nai.

Page26
1. Attakakatta. It was warm.
2. Karakatta. It was spicy.
3. Tanoshikatta. It was fun.
4. Ookikatta. It was big.
5. Muzukashikatta. It was difficult.
6. Takakatta. It was expensive.
7. Yasashikatta. It was easy.
8. Amakatta. It was sweet.
9. Isogashikatta. (I) was busy.
10. Suzushikatta. It was cool.

1. Ano mondai wa yasashikatta desu.
2. Ano suupu wa atsukatta desu.
3. Kyoo wa suzushikatta desu.
4. Sensei wa yokatta desu.
5. Setsumei wa warukatta desu.

Page 27
6. Nihon no jisho wa takakatta desu.
7. Piza wa mazukatta desu.
8. Seetaa wa atatakakatta desu.
9. Yuubinkyoku wa tookatta desu.
10. Zasshi wa omoshirokatta desu.

1. Kyoo wa samui desu.
2. Otototi wa isogashikatta desu.

3. Kyonen wa samukatta desu.
4. Kinoo no tempura wa oishikatta desu.
5. Ima wa tanoshii desu.

1. Sono piza wa tsumetakatta desu.
2. Sono gakkoo wa ookii desu.
3. Sono hon wa yasui desu.
4. Sono seetaa wa atatakakatta desu.
5. Kinoo wa tanoshikatta desu.

Page 28
6. Sono suupu wa tsumetai desu.
7. Kyoo wa suzushikatta desu.
8. Sono onna no ko wa chiisai desu.
9. Sono yuubinkyoku wa tooi desu.
10. Sono mondai wa muzukashikatta desu.
11. Geemu wa tanoshii desu.
12. Sono sensei wa yasashikatta desu.
13. Sono sushi wa takakatta desu.
14. Doyoobi wa atsukatta desu.
15. Sono setsumei wa yokatta desu.
16. Sono shinbun wa furui desu.
17. Sono eiga wa omoshirokatta desu.
18. Sono yasai wa atarashii desu.
19. Hikooki wa hayai desu.
20. Sono terebi wa takakatta desu.

Page 29
1. tanoshiku arimasen deshita = wasn't fun
2. oishiku arimasen deshita = wasn't good
3. atatakaku arimasen deshita = wasn't warm
4. karaku arimasen deshita = wasn't hot
5. ookiku arimasen deshita = wasn't big
6. muzukashiku arimasen deshita = wasn't difficult
7. tooku arimasen deshita = wasn't far
8. yoku arimasen deshita = wasn't good
9. amaku arimasen deshita = wasn't sweet
10. suzushiku arimasen deshita = wasn't cool

1. The train wasn't fast (early).
2. That computer was not good.
3. Today was cool.
4. That radio wasn't inexpensive
5. American magazines aren't interesting.
6. The fish was old.
7. That fruit wasn't sweet.
8. This car is not small.
9. That meat wasn't fresh.

Page 30
10. This coat is not warm.

1. Kinoo wa samuku arimasen deshita.
2. (Sono) ocha wa atsuku arimasen deshita.
3. (Sono) mizu wa tsumetaku arimasen deshita.
4. Isogashiku arimasen deshita.
5. (Sono) bangumi wa omoshiroku arimasen deshita.
6. (Sono) sushi wa oishiku arimasen deshita.
7. (Sono) resutoran wa takaku arimasen deshita.
8. (Sono) densha wa osoku arimasen deshita.
9. (Sono) shinbun wa furuku arimasen deshita.
10. (Sono) uchi wa ookiku arimasen deshita.
11. Tenki wa waruku arimasen deshita.
12. (Sono) setsumei wa muzukashiku arimasen deshita.
13. (Sono) gakkoo wa chikaku arimasen deshita.
14. (Sono) neko wa chiisaku arimasen deshita.
15. (sono) mise wa yasuku arimasen deshita.
16. (Sono) terebi wa ookiku arimasen deshita.
17. (Sono) heya wa suzushiku arimasen deshita.

Page 31
18. (Sono) basu wa hayaku arimasen deshita.
19. (Sono) piza wa mazuku arimasen deshita.
20. Kinoo wa tanoshiku arimasen deshita.

1. Oishiku nakatta. It didn't taste good.
2. Ookiku nakatta. It wasn't big.
3. Inu wa chiisaku nakatta. (The) dog wasn't small
4. Amerika no eiga wa omoshiroku nakatta. (The) American movie wasn't interesting.
5. Tenki wa yoku nakatta. The weather wasn't good.
6. Kono karee wa karaku nakatta. This curry wasn't spicy.
7. Mondai wa muzukashiku nakatta. The problem wasn't difficult.
8. Suupu wa atsuku nakatta. (The) soup wasn't hot.
9. Kyoo wa suzushiku nakatta. Today wasn't cool.
10. Yuubinkyoku wa tooku nakatta. The post office wasn't far.

11. Niku wa atarashiku nakatta. (The) meat wasn't fresh.
12. Yasai wa yasuku nakatta. (The) vegetables weren't inexpensive.

Page 32

1. (Sono) koohii wa atsuku nakatta.
2. (Sono) shinbun wa takaku nakatta.
3. Sensei wa yoku nakatta.
4. Kyoo wa attakaku nakatta (atatakaku nakatta).
5. (Sono) jisho wa yasuku nakatta.
6. (Sono) yuubinkyoku wa tooku nakatta.
7. Gakkoo wa tanoshiku nakatta.
8. (Sono) pan wa atarashiku nakatta.
9. (Sono) kuruma wa hayaku nakatta.
10. (Sono) koora wa tsumetaku nakatta.
11. (Sono) konpyuuta wa furuku nakatta.
12. Tenki wa waruku nakatta.

Page 34

1. Totemo omoshiroi desu.
2. Zenzen isogashiku arimasen.
3. Amari oishiku nai.
4. Itsumo tanoshii desu.
5. Zenzen atsuku nai.
6. Tokidoki takai.
7. Zenzen muzukashiku arimasen.
8. Taitei suzushii desu.
9. Kanari attakai (atatakai).
10. Amari hayaku arimasen deshita.
11. Tokidoki yasui desu.
12. Totemo isogashikatta desu.
13. Amari yasashiku arimasen.
14. Kanari tookatta.
15. Tokidoki ii desu.
16. Kanari warukatta desu.
17. Itsumo ii desu.
18. Anmari furuku nai.
19. Kanari atarashii.

Page 35

20. Zenzen omoshiroku arimasen.
21. Chotto ookii desu.
22. Kanari samui (tsumetai, depending on context).
23. Itsumo takakatta.
24. Chotto furukatta desu.
25. Zenzen isogashiku nakatta.

Page 36

1. My Japanese teacher is strict.

Page 37

2. It was awesome!
3. The car was red.
4. Tokyo summers are very hot and humid.
5. My mother isn't young.
6. The explanation wasn't at all detailed.
7. That dog isn't scary.
8. Today's weather was fantastic.
9. The room isn't very dirty.
10. My head didn't hurt. (I didn't have a headache.)
11. That team is very strong.
12. This is unusual candy, isn't it?
13. Is the sky blue?
14. That road was dangerous.
15. The walls weren't white.

1. Iie. Kuroku arimasen.
2. Iie. Mushiatsuku arimasen deshita.
3. Iie. Mezurashiku arimasen.

Page 38

4. Iie. Itaku arimasen deshita.
5. Iie. Ureshiku arimasen.

Examples of correct responses.

1. Ano neko wa kawaiku nai.
2. Kinoo no tenki wa warukatta desu.
3. Kono kuruma wa totemo abunai.
4. Sono keshiki wa subarashikatta desu.
5. Toire wa kitanaku nakatta.

1. Totemo kitanakatta desu.
2. Ureshiku arimasen.
3. Kawaikatta desu.
4. Sabishiku arimasen deshita.
5. Abunaku arimasen.
6. Akakatta desu.

Page 39

1. Sugoi!
2. Mezurashiku nai.
3. Aoku nakatta.
4. Kanari kuwashikatta.
5. Zenzen kibishiku nai.

Page 40
1. Samuku arimasen.
   Samuku nai.
   Samuku nai desu.
   It's not cold.

Page 41
2. Tanoshiku arimasen.
   Tanoshiku nai.
   Tanoshiku nai desu.
   It's not fun.
3. Amaku arimasen.
   Amaku nai.
   Amaku nai desu.
   It's not sweet.
4. Atatakaku arimasen.
   Atatakaku nai.
   Atatakaku nai desu.
   It's not warm.
5. Osoku arimasen.
   Osoku nai.
   Osoku nai desu.
   It's not late (slow).

1. Muzukashiku arimasen deshita.
   Muzukashiku nakatta.
   Muzukashiku nakatta desu.
   It wasn't difficult.
2. Chikaku arimasen deshita.
   Chikaku nakatta.
   Chikaku nakatta desu.
   It wasn't near.

Page 42
3. Isogashiku arimasen deshita
   Isogashiku nakatta
   Isogashiku nakatta desu
   I wasn't busy.
4. Yoku arimasen deshita.
   Yoku nakatta.
   Yoku nakatta desu.
   It wasn't good.
5. Akaku arimasen deshita.
   Akaku nakatta.
   Akaku nakatta desu.
   It wasn't red.

Page 43
1. Oishiku nai deshoo.

Page 44
2. Oishii deshoo?
3. Oishii deshoo.
4. Oishikatta deshoo?
5. Oishiku nakatta deshoo.

1. It's cool today, isn't it?
2. It will probably be cool tomorrow too.
3. That movie wasn't interesting, was it?
4. Japan is probably beautiful.
5. Japanese isn't difficult, is it?
6. This water is cold, isn't it?
7. Tokyo was probably hot and humid.
8. Awesome, isn't it?
9. He's probably not busy now.
10. Planes are fast, aren't they?

Page 45
1. Yasashii deshoo.
   Yasashikatta deshoo.
   Yashikatta deshoo?
2. Mushiatsui deshoo.
   Mushiatsukatta deshoo?
   Mushiatsuku nai deshoo.
3. Omoshiroku nai deshoo?
   Omoshiroku nai deshoo.
   Omoshiroi deshoo.
4. Mazushii deshoo.
   Mazushii deshoo?
   Mazushiku nai deshoo?
5. Kibishikatta deshoo?
   Kibishiku nai deshoo.
   Kibishii deshoo?
6. Ureshii deshoo.
   Ureshiku nai deshoo.
   Ureshikatta deshoo.

Page 46
7. Sabishii deshoo.
   Sabishishikatta deshoo.
   Sabishiku nakatta deshoo.
8. Shiroi deshoo?
   Shiroku nakatta deshoo?
   Shirokatta deshoo.

1. Ureshii deshoo?
2. Kibishii deshoo.
3. Omoshirokatta deshoo?
4. Itaku nai deshoo.

5. Samui deshoo.
6. Takakatta deshoo.

Page 47

7. Atsukatta deshoo?
8. Isogashiku nai deshoo.

Page 48

1. Iie. Takaku wa nakatta desu. No. It wasn't really expensive.

Page 49

2. Iie. Oishiku wa arimasen. No. It's not really what I'd call delicious.
3. Iie. Muzukashiku wa nai desu. No. I wouldn't say it's difficult.
4. Iie. Omoshiroku wa arimasen. No. I wouldn't say that it's interesting.
5. Iie. Isogashiku wa arimasen deshita. No. I wouldn't say that I was busy.
6. Iie. Atsuku wa nakatta desu. No. It wasn't quite what you'd call hot.
7. Iie. Hiroku wa nai desu. No. I wouldn't say it is large.
8. Iie. Tsumetaku wa nai desu. No. It's not really cold.
9. Iie. Tooku wa nai desu. No. It's not really far.
10. Iie. Waruku wa nai desu. No. She's not what one would call bad.
11. Iie. Atarashiku wa nai desu. No. They're not really what one could call fresh.

Page 50

12. Iie. Yasuku wa nai desu. No. It's not really what you could call inexpensive.
13. Iie. Omoshiroku wa nakatta desu. No. It wasn't really interesting.
14. Iie. Furuku wa nai desu. No. It's not really old.
15. Iie. Hayaku wa nakatta desu. No. It wasn't what one could call fast.

Page 51

1. Atsui soo desu. / Atsuku nai soo desu. / Atsukatta soo desu. / Atsuku nakatta soo desu.
2. Isogashii soo desu. / Isogashikatta soo desu.

Page 52

2. (cont'd) Isogashiku nakatta soo desu. / Isogashiku nai soo desu.
3. Atarashii soo desu. / Atarashiku nakatta soo desu. / Atarashiku nai soo desu. / Atarashikatta soo desu.
4. Takai soo desu. / Takaku nai soo desu. / Takaku nakatta soo desu. / Takakatta soo desu.
5. Yoku nakatta soo desu. / Yoku nai soo desu. / Yokatta soo desu. / Ii soo desu.

1. I hear that restaurant is very good.
2. I understand that that magazine was not interesting at all.
3. I hear that the test is very difficult.

Page 53

4. I understand that those shoes aren't very good.
5. I understand that the weather will be good.
6. I heard that the movie tickets were inexpensive.

1. Kyoo wa totemo isogashii soo desu.
2. Totemo takai soo desu.
3. Kippu wa yasuku nakatta soo desu.
4. Nihon wa anmari atsuku nai soo desu.
5. Uchi wa anmari hiroku nai soo desu.
6. Shiken wa zenzen muzukashiku nakatta soo desu.
7. Yasai wa anmari atarashiku nai soo desu.
8. Kuruma wa furukatta soo desu.
9. Totemo tanoshikatta soo desu.
10. Densha wa anmari hayaku nai soo desu.

Page 54

1. atsuku 2. omoshiroku 3. kibishiku
4. amaku 5. hayaku 6. Isogashiku
7. tanoshiku 8. akaku 9. mazushiku
10. tooku 11. ookiku 12. yasuku

Page 55

13. yoku 14. chikaku 15. suzushiku
16. yasashiku 17. karaku 18. oishiku
19. atarashiku 20. waruku

1. Samuku narimashita.
2. Yasuku narimashita.

3. Omoshiroku narimashita.
4. Yasashiku narimasu.
5. Akaku narimashita.
6. Tanoshiku narimasu.
7. Utsukushiku narimashita.

Page 56
8. Isogashiku narimashita.
9. Yoku narimashita.
10. Kitanaku narimasu.
11. Suzushiku narimasu.
12. Urusaku narimashita.
13. Nihongo wa muzukashiku narimashita.
14. Sensei wa kibishiku narimashita.
15. Mondai wa yasashiku narimashita.
16. Kuruma wa furuku narimashita.
17. Atatakaku narimasu.
18. Tenki wa waruku narimashita.
19. Koohii wa tsumetaku narimashita.
20. Sabishiku narimashita.

1. Atsuku shimasu.

Page 57
2. Yasuku shimashita.
3. Omoshiroku shimashita.
4. Hayaku shimasu.
5. Sensei wa muzukashiku shimashita.
6. Chiisaku shimasu ka?
7. Tanoshiku shimashita.
8. Karaku shimashita.

Page 58
1. We got up early.
2. He came late.
3. They worked busily.
4. They sold the car at a high price.
5. The teacher taught us sternly.
6. I went to bed early.
7. We rebuilt the house (built the house new)
8. The teacher explained it in a detailed fashion.

1. Yasuku urimashita.
2. Osoku kimashita.
3. Hayaku nemashita.
4. Kuwashiku hanashimashita.
5. Yasashiku iimashita.
6. Yoku benkyoo shimashita.

7. Takaku kaimashita.

Page 59
8. Tanoshiku asobimashita.
9. Kibishiku iimashita.
10. Osoku okimashita.

Page 60
1. takakute 2. atsukute 3. mezurashikute
4. oishikute 5. chikakute 6. kitanakute
7. suzushikute

Page 61
8. tanoshikute 9. yokute 10. furukute

1. atsukute 2. omoshirokute 3. atarashikute
4. osokute 5. oishikute 6. chiisakute
8. warukute 8. tookute 9. atatakakute
10. utsushikute 11. yasukute 12. Isogashikute

Page 62
1. Kore wa atarashikute ii desu.
2. Kono koohii wa atsukute oishii desu.
3. Kono resutoran wa takakute mazukatta desu.
4. Ano inu wa chiisakute kawaii desu.
5. Kono kuruma wa furukute yoku arimasen
6. Kono niku wa yasukute atarashikute oishii desu.

Page 63
1. The sushi was good so I ate a lot.
2. Yesterday I was busy and so it was rough going.
3. That dog is big and eats a lot.
4. That movie was interesting so I saw it twice.
5. This park is fun and so I come everyday.

1. Mizu wa tsumetakute oishii desu.
2. (Sono) konpyuuta wa furukute yoku nai desu.
3. Ano resutoran wa yasukute oishii desu.
4. Me ga akakute itai desu.
5. (Sono) sensei wa wakakute utsukushii desu.
6. Ano piza wa oishikute mainichi tabemashita.
7. Ookikute aoi desu.
8. Mezurashikute omoshiroi desu.
9. (Sono) tokei wa chiisakute takai desu.

Page 64
10. Furukute oishiku nai desu.

11. (Sono) basu wa osokute kitanai desu.
12. (Sono) neko wa chiisakute kawaii desu.

Page 65
1. ookiku nai	ookiku nakute
2. mazuku nai	mazuku nakute
3. tooku nai	tooku nakute
4. urusaku nai	urusaku nakute
5. atatakaku nai	atatakaku nakute
6. aoku nai	aoku nakute
7. isogashiku nai	isogashiku nakute
8. kuroku nai	kuroku nakute
9. sabishiku nai	sabishikunakute
10. samuku nai	samuku nakute

Page 66
11. chikaku nai	chikaku nakute
12. kawaiku nai	kawaiku nakute
13. yoku nai	yoku nakute
14. yasashiku nai	yasashiku nakute
15. suzushiku nai	suzushiku nakute

1. chiisa kunakute
2. yasuku nakute
3. muzukashiku nakute
4. omoshiroku nakute
5. sabishiku nakute
6. suzushiku nakute
7. mazuku nakute
8. takaku nakute
9. tanoshiku nakute
10. mezurashiku nakute
11. furuku nakute
12. waruku nakute

Page 67
13. yasashiku nakute
14. amaku nakute
15. abunaku nakute

1. (Sono) kuruma wa furuku nakute yokatta desu.
2. (Sono) biiru wa tsumetaku nakute oishiku nai desu.
3. (Sono) niku wa atarashiku nakute oishiku arimasen.
4. (Sono) jisho wa ookiku nakute ii desu.
5. Kyoo wa atsuku nakute yokatta desu.

Page 68
1. furukute chiisai uchi
2. yasukute omoshiroi zasshi
3. tsumetakute oishii koora
4. omoshirokute ii hito
5. chikakute ii gakkoo
6. ookikute chikai kooen
7. chiisakute kawaii onna no ko
8. yasashikute omoshiroi hon
9. ookikute kuroi inu
10. kitanakute chiisai heya

Page 69
(examples of correct answers)
1. ookikute tsuyoi hito
2. ookikute kowai inu
3. tsumetakute oishii beer
4. atatakakute takai seetaa
5. mazushikute sabishii hito
6. furukute warui kuruma
7. wakakute utsukushii hito
8. atarashikute hayai densha

Page 70
1. It is a large but dirty room.
2. It's an old but good car.
3. Although not hot, it's delicious coffee.
4. She's a strict but good teacher.
5. It's a large but cute dog.

1. Tsumetai desu ga oishii koohii desu.
2. Chiisai desu ga ii kooen desu.
3. Chiisai desu ga kowai neko desu.
4. Muzukashii desu ga omoshiroi hon desu.
5. Takai desu ga omoshiroi zasshi desu.
6. Ookii desu ga, yoku nai yuubinkyoku desu.
7. Takai desu ga ii kutsu desu.
8. Yasui desu ga oishii biiru desu.

Page 71
9. Oishiku nai desu ga yasui sushi desu.
10. Kuwashii desu ga muzukashii setsumei desu.

1. Atsukute oishii koohii desu.
2. Ookii desu ga kawaii inu desu.
3. Ookii desu ga furui uchi desu.
4. Ookii desu ga kitanai kooen desu.
5. Chikakute ii gakkoo desu.
6. Kibishii desu ga ii sensei desu.

7. Omoshiroku nai desu ga takai zasshi desu.

8. Furui desu ga ii tokei desu.

9. Atatakakute yasui seetaa desu.

10. Yasukute oishii sushi desu.

Page 72

1. Is it OK if the coffee is cold?

2. Is it all right if the books aren't interesting?

3. Is it all right if the problems are difficult?

4. Is it OK if the weather isn't good?

1. Yasashikute mo ii desu ka?

2. Biiru wa tsumetaku nakute mo ii desu ka?

Page 73

3. Konpyuuta wa atarashiku nakute mo ii desu ka?

4. Kami wa shirokute mo ii desu ka?

5. Gakkoo wa tookute mo ii desu ka?

6. Setsumei wa kuwashiku nakute mo ii desu ka?

7. Pen wa akakute mo ii desu ka?

8. Atatakaku nakute mo ii desu ka?

9. Kitanakute mo ii desu ka?

10. Osokute mo ii desu ka?

1. Chiisakute mo ii desu.

2. Koohii wa tsumetakute mo ii desu.

3. Shinbun wa furukute mo ii desu.

4. Kippu wa takakute mo ii desu.

5. Pen wa kuroku nakute mo ii desu.

6. Yasai wa atarashiku nakute mo ii desu.

7. Uchi wa kitanakute mo ii desu.

8. Neko wa kawaiku nakute mo ii desu.

9. Tenki wa warukute mo ii desu.

10. Karee wa karaku nakute mo ii desu.

Page 74

1. Takakute mo ii.

2. Atsukute mo kamaimasen ka?

3. Tsumetaku nakute mo ii no?

4. Samukute mo ii desu.

5. Furukute mo ii desu ka?

6. Atarashiku nakute mo ii.

7. Omoshiroku nakute mo ii desu ka?

8. Yoku nakute mo kamaimasen.

9. Akakute mo kamaimasen ka?

10. Chikaku nakute mo ii desu.

Page 75

1. Iie. Furukute wa ikemasen.

2. Iie. Yasahikute wa dame desu.

3. Iie. Kurokute wa ikemasen.

4. Iie. Akakute wa dame desu.

5. Iie. Yasukute wa ikemasen.

6. Iie. Ookikute wa dame desu.

Page 76

1. Takakute mo kamaimasen ka?

Takakute wa ikemasen ka?

Takakute mo ii desu ka?

Takakute mo ii?

2. Biiru wa tsumetaku nakute mo kamaimasen ka?

Biiru wa tsumetaku nakute wa ikemasen ka?

Biiru wa tsumetaku nakute mo ii (ka)?

Biiru wa tsumetaku nakute mo ii no?

3. Atarashiku nakute mo kamaimasen ka?

Atarashiku nakute mo ii desu ka?

Atarashiku nakute wa dame desu ka?

Atarashiku nakute mo ii no?

4. Karee wa karakute mo kamaimasen ka?

Karee wa karakute wa ikemasen ka?

Karee wa karakute mo ii desu ka?

Karee wa karakute wa dame desu ka?

Page 77

5. Shiroku nakute wa ikemasen ka?

Shiroku nakute mo ii desu ka?

Shiroku nakute ii (ka)?

Shiroku nakute ii no?

Page 78

1. samukereba 2. chiisakereba 3. tsuyokereba

4. urusakereba 5. yokereba 6. tanoshikereba

7. hayakereba

Page 79

8. atatakakereba 9. mazushikereba

10. aokereba 11. isogashikereba

12. kuwashikereba 13. muzukashikereba

14. chikakereba 15. warukereba 16. osokereba

17. yasashikereba 18. kitanakereba

19. ookikereba 20. furukereba

1. Tookereba 2. chiisakereba 3. yokereba

4. chikakereba 5. yasukereba 6. yasashikereba

Page 80

7. isogashikereba 8. suzushikereba

9. sabishikereba 10. tanoshikereba

11. atarashikereba 12. hayakereba

13. osokereba 14. oishikereba
15. ureshikereba

1. Chikakereba ii desu.
2. Koohii ga atsukereba ii desu.
3. Tenki ga yokereba ii desu.
4. Yasukereba ii desu.

Page 81
5. Chiisakereba ii desu.
6. Atatakakereba ii desu.
7. Chikaereba ii desu.
8. Shirokereba ii desu.
9. Tanoshikereba ii desu.
10. Ureshikereba ii desu.

1. tabemasu. If the sushi is good, I'll eat it.
2. kaimasu. If the magazine is cheap, I'll buy it.
3. sooji shimasu. If the rooms are dirty, I'll clean them.

Page 82
4. tetsudaimasu. If you're busy, I'll helPage
5. yomimasu. If the book is easy, I'll read it.
6. ikimasu. If the weather is good, we'll go.
7. deeto shimasu. If he's nice, I'll go on a date [with him].
8. kikimasu. If the music is good, I'll listen to it.
9. nomimasu. If the coffee is hot, I'll drink it.
10. mimasu. If the TV show is interesting, we'll watch it.

1. Tenki ga yokereba ikimasu.
2. Omoshirokereba kikimasu.
3. Yasashikereba yomimasu.
4. Yasukereba kaimasu.
5. Oishikereba tabemasu.
6. Yashikereba deeto o shimasu.
7. Kitanakereba sooji shimasu.
8. Isogashikereba tetsudaimasu.

Page 83
9. Omoshirokereba mimasu.
10. Tsumetakereba nomimasu.

1. The more difficult the problem, the more interesting it is.
2. The larger the diamond, the more expensive it is.

3. The older the violin, the more expensive it is.
4. The hotter the soup is, the tastier it is.
5. The colder the beer, the better [it tastes].
6. The fresher the vegetables, the better [tasting] they are.

Page 84
1. muzukashikereba muzukashii hodo
2. chiisakereba chiisai hodo
3. takakereba takai hodo
4. oishikereba oishii hodo
5. kibishikereba kibishii hodo
6. isogashikereba isogashii hodo
7. ookikereba ookii hodo
8. atarashikereba atarashii hodo
9. omoshirokereba omoshiroi hodo
10. yasashikereba yasashii hodo
11. karakereba karai hodo
12. amakereba amai hodo

1. Hayakereba hayai hodo ii desu.
2. Karee raisu wa karakereba karai hodo oishii desu.
3. Suupu wa atsukereba atsui hodo oishii desu.
4. Sensei wa kibishikereba kibishii hodo ii desu.

Page 85
5. Kuruma wa atarashikereba atarashii hodo ii desu.
6. Shiken wa yasashikereba yasashii hodo ii desu.
7. Daiya wa ookikereba ookii hodo ii desu.
8. Konpyuuta wa atarashikereba atarashii hodo takai desu.
9. Kuruma wa furukereba furui hodo yasui desu.
10. Shigoto wa isogashikereba isogashii hodo ii desu.
11. Eiga wa furukereba furui hodo omoshiroi desu.
12. Setsumei wa kuwashikereba kuwashii hodo ii desu.

Page 86
1. mazuku nakereba 2. tsumetaku nakereba
3. osoku nakereba 4. tooku nakereba
5. tanoshiku nakereba 6. ookiku nakereba
7. oishiku nakereba 8. yoku nakereba
9. urusaku nakereba 10. tsuyoku nakereba

11. ureshiku nakereba 12. chiisaku nakereba
13. atarashiku nakereba

Page 87
14. yasuku nakereba 15. muzukashiku nakereba
16. kuroku nakereba 17. furuku nakereba
18. takaku nakereba 19. kawaiku nakereba
20. kowaku nakereba

1. Chikaku nakereba 2. Akaku nakereba
3. Atarashiku nakereba 4. Kowaku nakereba
5. Isogashiku nakereba 6. Yasashiku nakereba
7. Tooku nakereba 8. Kitanaku nakereba
9. Utsukushiku nakereba
10. Atatakaku nakereba

Page 88
1. Atsuku nakereba irimasen.
2. Chiisakereba irimasen.
3. Muzukashiku nakereba irimasen.
4. Yasashikereba irimasen.
5. Atatakaku nakereba irimasen.
6. Kitanakereba irimasen.
7. Oishiku nakereba irimasen.
8. Takakereba irimasen.

Sample answers
1. Tenki ga yoku nakereba ikimasen.
2. Isogashiku nakereba benkyoo shimasu.
3. Takaku nakereba kaimasu.
4. Muzukashiku nakereba yomimasu.

Page 89
1. Kurokunakereba narimasen.
2. Chikakunakereba narimasen.
3. Atsuku nakereba narimasen.
4. Omoshiroku nakereba narimasen.
5. Aoku nakereba narimasen.
6. Yoku nakereba narimasen.
7. Isogashiku nakereba narimasen.
8. Atarashiku nakereba narimasen.
9. Yasuku nakereba narimasen.
10. Hayaku nakereba narimasen.
11. Chiisaku nakereba narimasen.
12. Tsuyoku nakereba narimasen.

1. Sensei wa kibishiku narakereba narimasen.
2. Tenki ga yoku nakereba narimasen.
3. Chiimu wa tsuyoku nakereba narimasen.

4. Zasshi wa omoshiroku nakereba
narimasen.

Page 90
1. oishisoo 2. mazusoo 3. chiisasoo
4. kibishisoo 5. itasoo 6. takasoo 7. yosasoo
8. tsuyosoo 9. furusoo 10. omoshirosoo
11. samusoo

Page 91
12. suzushisoo 13. ureshisoo 14. sabishisoo
15. yasashisoo

1. Samusoo desu. 2. Sabishisoo desu.
3. Itasoo desu. 4. Ureshisoo desu.
5. Kibishisoo desu. 6. Tsuyosoo desu.
7. Oishisoo desu. 8. Furusoo desu.

Page 92
9. Isogashisoo desu. 10. Yosasoo desu.

1. Tsumetasoo desu.
2. Tsuyosoo desu.
3. Ureshisoo desu.
4. Sabishisoo desu.
5. Muzukashisoo desu.
6. Furusoo desu.
7. Kibishisoo desu.

Page 93
1. oishisoo na ryoori
2. tsuyosoo na otoko no hito
3. kibishisoo na sensei
4. atatakasoo na seetaa
5. tsumetasoo na mizu
6. abunasoo na michi
7. yasashisoo na onna no hito
8. ureshisoo na kodomo
9. muzukashisoo na mondai
10. takasoo na doresu
11. sabishisoo na hito

Page 94
1. I think that Ms. Sasaki is busy.
2. I think that sushi was bad tasting.
3. I think that that post office is not very far.
4. I think that it was very cold yesterday.
5. I think that these vegetables don't taste
good.

Page 95

1. Atsui to omoimasu.
2. Yokatta to omoimasu.
3. Tooku nai to omoimasu.
4. Uchi wa chikakatta to omoimasu.
5. Kippu wa amari takaku nakatta to omoimasu.
6. Kyoo wa isogashiku nai to omoimasu.
7. (Sono) uchi wa kanari chiisai to omoimasu.
8. Tenki wa taitei atatakai to omoimasu.
9. Tenki wa waruku nakatta to omoimasu.
10. (Sono) gakkoo wa ookikatta to omoimasu.
11. Basu wa hayaku nai to omoimasu.
12. (Sono) niku wa atarashiku nakatta to omoimasu.
13. Osoku nai to omoimasu.
14. Shiken wa yasashikatta to omoimasu.
15. (Sono) kuruma wa kanari atarashikatta to omoimasu.

Page 96

Hoshii desu. / Hoshii.
Hoshiku arimasen. / Hoshiku nai.

Page 97

Hoshikatta desu. / Hoshikatta.
Hoshiku arimsen deshita. / Hoshiku nakatta.

1. Pan ga hoshikatta desu.
2. Atarashii kuruma wa hoshiku nai.
3. Karaa terebi ga hoshikatta desu.
4. Shinbun wa hoshiku nakatta desu.
5. Atarashi yasai ga hoshikatta.
6. Kuwashii setsumei wa hoshiku nai desu.
7. Sushi wa hoshiku nakatta desu.
8. Nani ga hoshii desu ka?
9. (Sono) akai kutsu ga hoshikatta.
10. Kuroi shatsu wa hoshiku arimasen.
11. Zenzen hoshiku arimasen.
12. Anmari hoshiku nai.
13. Koohii wa hoshiku nakatta.
14. Tempura ga hoshikatta?
15. Atarashii konpyuuta wa hoshiku nai.

1. kuro no kaban 2. kiiro no doresu

Page 99

3. aoi shatsu 4. shiro no kami
5. akai seetaa

Page 100

1. chairo no kaban 2. akashingoo
3. pinku no hana 4. kon no suutsu
5. guree no sukaato 6. rabendaa no seetaa
7. aoshingoo 8. beeju no doresu 9. aozora
10. guriin ken

1. kuro to beeju no seetaa
2. rabendaa to aka no sokkusu

Page 101

3. chairo to shiro no inu
4. ao to pinku no suutsu
5. aka to kiiro no nekutai
6. kuro to beeju no sukaato
7. aka to kuro no kaban
8. kiiro to pinku no shatsu

1. Kiiro ga suki desu.
2. Chairo ga ii desu.
3. Pinku ga suki desu.
4. Ao ga ii desu.
5. Rabendaa ga suki desu ka?
6. Kuro ga ii desu ka?

Page 102

7. Guree to chairo ga suki desu ka?
8. Ao to shiro wa ii desu.
9. Aka to shiro to ao ga suki desu.
10. Guriin to shiro wa ii desu ka?

Page 103

1. Shiroppoi desu ka?
2. Shiroppoku arimasen.
3. Shiroppokatta.
4. Shiroppoku arimasen deshita.
5. Shiroppoku nai.
6. Shiroppoku narimashita.

1. akappoi
2. shiroppoi

Page 104

3. kiiroppoi
4. aoppoi
5. kuroppoi

1. a kind of black (blackish) dog
2. a reddish sweater

3. a kind of blue (bluish) skirt
4. a brownish color bag
5. a whitish building
6. a yellowish sky
7. a flushed (red) face

1. Kuroppoi inu o mimashita.
2. Sora wa kiiropokatta desu.
3. Chairoppoku narimashita.
4. Akappoi seetaa o kaimashita.
5. Shiroppoi biru desu.

Page 105
1. muzukashisa 2. ookisa 3. mezurashisa
4. oishisa 5. atarashisa

Page 106
6. kibishisa 7. wakasa 8. sabishisa 9. itasa
10. mazushisa

1. Sore wa isogashisa ni yorimasu.
2. Sore wa mondai no muzukashisa ni yorimasu.
3. Sore wa uchi no ookisa ni yorimasu.
4. Sore wa samusa ni yorimasu.
5. Sore wa kuruma no atarashisa ni yorimasu.
6. Sore wa hon no omoshirosa ni yorimasu.
7. Sore wa densha no hayasa ni yorimasu.
8. Sore wa okashi no amasa ni yorimasu.
9. Sore wa setsumei no kuwashiwa ni yorimasu.

Page 107
10. Sore wa terebi no yosa ni yorimasu.

1. Sore wa uchi no ookisa ni yorimasu.
2. Sore wa isogashisa ni yorimasu.
3. Sore wa okashi no oishisa ni yorimasu.
4. Sore wa karee no karasa ni yorimasu.
5. Sore wa hon no muzukashisa ni yorimasu.

1. Samusa ni bikkuri shimashita.
2. Nihon no atsusa ni bikkuri shimashita.
3. Shiken no muzukashisa ni bikkuri shimashita.
4. (Sono) chiimu no tsuyosa ni bikkuri shimasu.
5. (Sono) uchi no ookisa ni bikkuri shimashita.

6. (Sono) terebi no furusa ni bikkuri shimashita.

Page108
7. Kippu no yasusa ni bikkuri shimashita.
8. Shinkansen no hayasa ni bikkuri shimashita.
9. Atusa ni bikkuri shimashita.
10. Mizu no tsumetasa ni bikkuri shimashita.

Page 109
1. Atsukattari samukattari shimasu. /
Sometimes it's hot and sometimes cold.
2. Ookikattari chiisakattari shimasu. /
Sometimes they're big and sometimes they're small.
3. Tookattari chikakattari shimasu. /
Sometimes it's far and at other times it's near.

Page 110
4. Atarashikattari furukattari shimasu. /
At times they're new and at others they're old.
5. Kurokattari shirokattari shimasu. /
Sometimes it's black and sometimes it's white.
6. Yokattari warukattari shimasu. /
Sometimes they're good and sometimes they're bad.
7. Takakattari yasukattari shimasu. /
Sometimes they're expensive and sometimes they're cheap.
8. Amakattari karakattari shimasu. /
Sometimes they're sweet and sometimes they're spicy.

1. Japanese houses can be small or big.
2. The teacher is sometimes kind and sometimes stern.
3. The restaurant's tempura is sometimes good and sometimes bad.
4. Winters can be cold or warm.
5. The train is sometimes early and sometimes late.

1. Takakattari yasukattari shimasu.
2. Ookikattari chiisakattari shimasu.
3. Chikakattari tookattari shimasu.

Page 111

4. Natsu wa suzushikattari atsukattari shimasu.
5. Basu wa hayakattari osokattari shimasu.
6. Yasai wa atarashikattari furukattari shimasu.
7. Sabishikattari shimasu.
8. Koohii wa oishikattari mazukattari shimasu.
9. Karee raisu wa karakattari amakattari shimasu.
10. Nihonjin no sensei wa kibishikattari yasashikattari shimasu.
11. Shiken wa muzukashikattari yasashikattari shimasu.
12. Tenki ga yokattari warukattari shimasu.

1. Atsukattari atsuku nakattari shimasu.
2. Isogashikattari isogashiku nakattari shimasu.
3. Tanoshikattari tanoshiku nakattari shimasu.
4. Takakattari takaku nakattari shimasu.
5. Basu wa hayakattari hayaku nakattari shimasu.
6. Shiken wa muzukashikattari muzukashiku nakattari shimasu.

Page 112

7. Inu wa ookikattari ookiku nakattari shimasu.
8. Pan wa atarashikattari atarashiku nakattari shimasu.
9. Ryoori wa oishikattari oishiku nakattari shimasu.
10. Hon wa omoshirokattari omoshiroku nakattari shimasu.
11. Shiken wa yasashikattari yasashiku nakattari shimasu.
12. Tekisuto wa yasukattari yasuku nakattari shimasu.

1. Muzukashikattari yasashikattari shimasu.
2. Ookikattari chisakattari shimasu.
3. Oishikattari mazukattari shimasu.
4. Yasukattari yasuku nakattari shimasu.
5. Kibishikattari yasashikattari shimasu.
6. Yasashikattari yasashiku nakattari shimasu.
7. Omoshirokattari omoshiroku nakattari shimasu.
8. Hayakattari osokattari shimasu.

Page 113

1. Samusugimasu.
2. Atsusugimashita.
3. Kibishisugimasu.
4. Urusasugimashita.
5. Furusugimasu.
6. (Sono) doresu wa yasusugimasu.
7. (Sono) mondai wa muzukashisugimasu.
8. Fuyu wa samusugimasu.

Page 114

9. (Sono) karee raisu wa karasugimasu.
10. (Sono) keeki wa amasugimasu.
11. (Sono) jisho wa furusugimasu.
12. (Sono) sensei wa wakasugimasu.
13. (Sono) uchi wa chiisasugimashita.
14. (Sono) koohii wa mazusugimasu.
15. (Sono) koora wa tsumetasugimasu.

1. Chotto ookisugimasu.
2. Chotto tsumetasugimasu.
3. Chotto kibishisugimasu.
4. Chotto yasashisugimashita.
5. Chotto ookisugimasu.
6. Chotto chiisasugimasu.
7. Chotto furusugimashita.
8. Chotto samusugimasu.

Page 115

9. Chotto atsusugimasu.
10. Chotto isogashisugimasu.

1. Toosugiru to omoimasu.
2. Biiru wa tsumetasugiru to iimashita.
3. (Sono) shiken wa yasashisugiru to omoimasu.
4. (Sono) seetaa wa chiisasugiru to iimashita.
5. Hokkaidoo wa samusugiru to omoimasu.
6. (Sono) kutsu wa takasugiru to iimashita.
7. (Sono) jisho wa furusugiru to omoimasu.
8. (Sono) kusuri wa tsuyosugiru to iimashita.
9. (Sono) uchi wa toosugiru to omoimasu.
10. (Sono) densha wa ososugiru to iimashita.

Page 117

1. ki ga ookii hito
2. kuchi ga warui hito
3. sei ga takai hito
4. kimochi ga ii hi

5. mimi ga tooi hito
6. hana ga takai hito
7. atama ga ii kodomo
8. ki ga chiisai hito
9. ashi ga hayai hito
10. kimochi ga warui eiga

Page 118
1. Haha wa me ga ookii desu.
2. Kyoo wa kimochi ga ii hi desu.
3. Tomodachi wa mimi ga tooi desu.
4. (Sono) joyuu wa kuchi ga chiisai desu.
5. (Sono) sensei wa kuchi ga warui desu.
6. Tomoko-san wa sei ga takai desu.
7. Akira-san wa totemo atama ga ii desu.
8. Tanaka-san wa ki ga ookii desu.
9. Kono heya wa kimochi ga ii desu.
10. Matsuyama-san wa ki ga chiisai desu.

Sample answers
1. Sei ga hikui desu.
2. Atama ga ii hito desu.
3. Kimochi ga ii desu.
4. Hana ga takai desu.
5. Sei ga takai hito desu.
6. Kuchi ga warui desu.

Page 119
1. Paatii ni hito ga ookatta desu.
2. Paatii ni hito ga ooku arimasen.

Page 120
3. Paatii ni hito ga ooku nakatta desu.
4. Paatii ni hito ga ooku nakereba narimasen
5. Tomodachi wa ooi to iimashita.
6. Paatii ni hito ga ookute mo ii desu.
7. Paatii ni hito ga ooku nakatta deshoo
8. Paatii ni hito ga ooku nai to omoimasu.
9. Paatii ni hito ga ooi deshoo?
10. Paatii ni hito ga ookute tanoshikatta desu.

1. Paati ni tabemono ga sukunakatta.
2. Paati ni tabemono ga sukunaku nakatta desu.
3. Paati ni tabemono ga sukunaku arimasen.
4. Paati ni tabemono ga sukunai to omoimasu.
5. Tomodachi wa paati ni tabemono ga sukunai to iimashita.
6. Paati ni tabemono ga sukunai deshoo?

7. Paati ni tabemono ga sukunakatta soo desu.
8. Paati ni tabemono ga sukunakute mo ii desu.

Page 121
9. Paatii ni tabemono ga sukunakute tanoshiku nakatta desu.
10. Paati ni tabemono ga sukunasasoo desu.

1. ooku no nihonjin 2. takusan no hon
3. ooku no kuni 4. ooku no machi
5. takusan no neko 6. ooku no gakusei
7. ooku no daigaku 8. takusan no shoosetsu

Page 122
9. ooku no sensei 10. ooku no kodomo
11. takusan no enpitsu 12. ooku no hito

Page 123
1. Atarashii hoo ga ii desu.
2. Yasuku nai hoo ga ii desu.
3. Koohii wa atsui hoo ga ii desu.
4. Konpyuuta wa atarashii hoo ga ii desu.
5. Jisho wa furuku nai hoo ga ii desu.
6. Kutsu wa takai hoo ga ii desu.
7. Karee raisu wa karai hoo ga ii desu.

Page 124
8. Sake wa atsui hoo ga ii desu.
9. Setsumei wa kuwashii hoo ga ii desu.
10. Sensei wa kibishiku nai hoo ga ii desu.
11. Ryoori wa mezurashii hoo ga ii desu.
12. Uchi wa chiisai hoo ga ii desu.

Sample answers
1. Iie. Chiisai hoo ga ii desu.
2. Iie. Furuku nai hoo ga ii desu.
3. Iie. Muzukashii hoo ga ii desu.
4. Iie. Ookii hoo ga ii desu.
5. Iie. Kibishii hoo ga ii desu.
6. Iie. Atsui hoo ga ii desu.

Page 125
7. Iie. Osoku nai hoo ga ii desu.
8. Iie. Chikai hoo ga ii desu.
9. Iie. Kuroi hoo ga ii desu.
10. Iie. Kuwashiku nai hoo ga ii desu.

1. Hot coffee tastes better.
2. Old movies are more interesting.
3. I prefer cold beer.
4. I prefer beer that's not too cold.
5. I prefer small cars.
6. Fresh sashimi tastes better.
7. New computers are more expensive.
8. Curry rice tastes better if it's not too spicy.

Page 126
1. Juusu wa tsumetai hoo ga oishii desu.
2. Mondai wa muzukashii hoo ga omoshiroi desu.
3. Kuruma wa ookii hoo ga suki desu.
4. Seetaa wa ookii hoo ga suki desu.
5. Keeki wa amaku nai hoo ga oishii desu.
6. O-cha wa atsui hoo ga oishii desu.
7. Uchi wa furui hoo ga omoshiroi desu.
8. Yasai wa atarashii hoo ga oishii desu.
9. Atarashii kuruma no hoo ga takai desu.
10. Hon wa furui hoo ga omoshiroi desu.
11. Gohan wa atsui hoo ga suki desu.
12. Suupu wa atsui hoo ga oishii desu.

Page 127
1. tooku no gakkoo
2. chikai tokoro
3. chikakute oishii kissaten

Page 128
4. tooi tokoro
5. Ano byooin wa chiisakute tooi desu.
6. chikaku no daigaku
7. tooku no toshokan
8. Ano depaato wa tooi desu ga, ii desu.
9. Chikai tokoro e ikimashita.
10. Chikakute oishii resutoran e ikimashita.
11. amari tooku nai suupaa
12. Chikai hoo ga ii desu.
13. Chikaku no kooen e ikimashita.
14. Resutoran wa chikaku nakute mo ii desu.
15. Gokko wa chikaku nakereba ikemasen.
16. Tooku nai hoo ga ii desu.
17. Chikai tokoro wa ii desu.
18. Kono chikaku de mimashita.

Page 132
1. raku 2. kirei 3. hen 4. shitsurei

5. hansamu 6. shinsetsu 7. modan
8. taisetsu 9. benri 10. shizuka 11. hima
12. fuben 13. dame 14. suteki 15. majime
16. tekitoo 17. anzen

Page 133
18. nigiyaka 19. rippa 20. teinei 21. . . . .

1. na lively 2. na convenient 3. i unusual
4. na healthy, energetic 5. na kind
6. na having free time 7. na famous
8. na chic 9. i good

Page 134
10. na stupid 11. i awesome 12. i blue
13. na safe 14. na various 15. na comfortable
16. na boring 17. na quiet 18. na inconvenient
19. na suitable 20. na refined

1. shizuka 2. omoshiroi

Page 135
3. benri 4. isogashii 5. ii 6. abunai
7. kitanai 8. teinei

1. hen, strange 2. shizuka, quiet
3. daijoobu, no problem 4. iroiro, various
5. yuumei, famous 6. baka stupid
7. taisetsu, precious 8. genki, healthy, energetic
9. tekitoo, appropriate 10. rippa, magnificent
11. hima, having free time 12. majime, diligent

Page 136
1. Shinsetsu desu. 2. Taikutsu desu.
3. Daijoobu desu. 4. Shizuka desu.
5. Benri desu. 6. Fuben desu
7. Anzen desu. 8. Hima desu.
9. Rippa desu. 10. Suteki desu.
11. Modan desu. 12. Tekitoo desu.

Page 137
13. Taisetsu desu. 14. Raku desu.
15. Teinei desu. 16. Benri desu.
17. Nigiyaka desu. 18. Dame desu.
19. Hen desu. 20. Yuumei desu.

1. Shizuka da. 2. Ookii. 3. Isogashii.
4. Yuumei da. 5. Taisetsu da.
6. Shitsurei da. 7. Tanoshii.

Page 138
8. Genki da. 9. Teinei da. 10. Daijoobu da.
11. Anzen da. 12. Suzushii. 13. Kuroi.
14. Hima da. 15. Dame da. 16. Tekitoo da.
17. Takai. 18. Tooi. 19. Baka da.
20. Suteki da.

1. Taikutsu ja arimasen.

Page 139
2. Anmari suteki ja arimasen.
3. Zenzen nigiyaka ja arimasen.
4. Anmari hansamu ja arimasen.
5. Amari teinei dewa arimasen.
6. Tookyoo wa anmari shizuka ja arimasen.
7. (Sono) isha wa amari shinsetsu ja arimasen.
8. (Sono) denwa wa dame ja arimasen.
9. (Sono) seetaa wa amari suteki ja arimasen.
10. (Sono) gakkoo wa anzen ja arimasen.
11. (Sono) eiga wa zenzen taikutsu ja arimasen.
12. Haha wa anmari genki ja arimasen.
13. (Sono) onna no hito wa joohin ja
    arimasen.
14. (Sono) heya wa kirei ja arimasen.
15. Hima ja arimasen.

Page 140
1. muzukashiku nai 2. majime ja nai
3. shitsurei ja nai 4. yasuku nai
5. taisetsu ja nai 6. rippa ja nai
7. fuben ja nai 8. modan ja nai
9. samuku nai 10. teinei ja nai
11. shizuka ja nai 12. suteki ja nai
13. tekitoo ja nai 14. raku ja nai
15. suzushiku nai 16. yoku nai
17. taisetsu ja nai 18. hima ja nai

Page 141
19. daijoobu ja nai 20. atarashiku nai

1. benri ja nai 2. tooku nai 3. shinsetsu da
4. kirei dewa nai 5. muzukashiku nai
6. shizuka ja arimasen 7. dame desu
8. nigiyaka da 9. omoshiroi 10. modan da.

Page 142
1. Taikutsu deshita. 2. Atatakakatta desu.
3. Daijoobu deshita. 4. Hansamu deshita.
5. Yuumei deshita. 6. Sabishikatta desu.

7. Oishikatta desu. 8. Anzen deshita.
9. Hen deshita. 10. Abunakatta desu.
11. Fuben deshita. 12. Tekitoo deshita.
13. Teinei deshita. 14. Hima deshita.
15. Raku deshita. 16. Majime deshita.
17. Nigiyaka deshita. 18. Dame deshita.
19. Kirei deshita. 20. Suteki deshita.

Page 143
1. raku deshita 2. shizuka datta
3. yuumei datta 4. samukatta desu.
5. mezurashikatta 6. daijoobu deshita
7. hima datta 8. taikutsu deshita
9. tekitoo datta 10. joohin deshita
11. baka datta 12. anzen deshita
13. nigiyaka deshita 14. hansamu datta
15. rippa datta 16. teinei deshita
17. hayakatta

Page 144
18. modan deshita 19. genki datta
20. iroiro deshita.

1. Shizuka ja arimasen deshita.
2. Hansamu ja arimasen deshita.
3. Takaku arimasen deshita.
4. Suteki ja arimasen deshita.
5. Tekitoo ja arimasen deshita.
6. Raku ja arimasen deshita.
7. Shitsurei ja arimasen deshita.
8. Atsuku arimasen deshita.
9. Isogashiku arimasen deshita.
10. Hima ja arimasen deshita.

Page 145
11. Teinei ja arimasen deshita
12. Taikutsu ja arimasen deshita
13. Omoshiroku arimasen deshita.
14. Yuumei ja arimasen deshita.
15. Benri ja arimasen deshita.
16. Joohin ja arimasen deshita.
17. Baka ja arimasen deshita.
18. Dame ja arimasen deshita.
19. Chikaku arimasen deshita.
20. Rippa ja arimasen deshita.

1. yasahiku nakatta 2. shinsetsu ja nakatta
3. taisetsu ja nakatta 4. benri ja nakatta
5. teinei ja nakatta

Page 146
6. tanoshiku nakatta 7. nigiyaka ja naktta
8. yuumei ja nakatta 9. fuben ja nakatta
10. suteki ja nakatta 11. genki ja nakatta
12. yoku nakatta 13. raku ja nakatta
14. taikutsu ja nakatta 15. majime ja nakatta

Page 147
1. Taisetsu ja nai desu.
2. Benri ja nakatta desu.
3. Kirei ja nai desu.
4. Yasuku nai desu.
5. Tooku nai desu.
6. Shizuka ja nakatta desu.
7. Tekitoo ja nai desu.
8. Yuumei ja nakatta desu.
9. Suteki ja nai desu.
10. Rippa ja nakatta desu.
11. Chiisaku nai desu.
12. Genki ja nai desu.

Page 148
13. Raku ja nakatta desu.
14. Nigiyaka ja nai desu.
15. anzen ja nai desu.

Page 149
1. Shizuka ja arimasen. 2. Shizuka da.
3. Shizuka deshita. 4. Shizuka ja nakatta desu.

1. Oishii. 2. Oishiku arimasen.
3. Oishiku nakatta. 4. Oishikatta desu.

1. Dame ja nakatta desu. 2. Dame deshita.
3. Dame ja nai. 4. Dame da.

1. Tekitoo desu. 2. Tekitoo ja nai.
3. Tekitoo datta. 4. Tekitoo ja arimasen deshita.

1. Taisetsu deshita. 2. Taisetsu ja nai desu
3. Taisetsu deshita. 4. Taisetsu ja arimasen
deshita.

Page 150
1. Tookyoo wa shizuka ja nakatta desu.
2. Kono uchi wa benri datta.
3. Kyoo wa atsukatta desu.
4. Sono isha wa shinsetsu ja nakatta desu.
5. Watashi wa baka ja arimasen.

Page 151
1. shizuka na machi 2. shinsetsu na kangofu

Page 152
3. hen na hi 4. isogashii hito 5. hima na hito
6. rippa na hito 7. taisetsu na tokei
8. tekitoo na tekisuto 9. atsui hi
10. taikutsu na eiga 11. shitsurei na ten-in
12. teinei na gakusei 14. iroiro na shinbun
15. ookii kuni 16. raku na seetaa
17. anzen na tokoro 18. abunai tokoro
19. yuumei na isha 21. benri na denwa
22. dame na denwa 23. nigiyaka na machi

Page 153
24. baka na gakusei 25. joohin na hito

1. Shinsetsu na isha ga imasu.
2. Omoshiroi eiga ga arimasu.
3. Tekitoo na tekisuto ga arimasu.
4. Taisetsu na tokei ga arimasu.
5. Suteki na onna no hito ga imasu.
6. Atsui koohii ga arimasu.

Page 154
7. Modan na biru ga arimasu.
8. Benri na mise ga arimasu.
9. Hansamu na otoko no hito ga imasu.
10. Iroiro na hito ga imasu.
11. Nigiyaka na machi ga arimasu.
12. Shizuka na kooen ga arimasu.
13. Teinei ga ten-in ga imasu.
14. Anzen na tokoro ga arimasu.
15. Ii gakusei ga imasu.

1. Omoshiroi eiga o mimashita.
2. Taikutsu na eiga o mimashita
3. Furui eiga o mimashita.

1. Yuumei na hito ni aimashita.
2. Shinsetsu na hito ni aimashita.
3. Ii hito ni aimashita.
4. Suteki na hito ni aimashita.

Page 155
1. Taikutsu na shoosetsu o yomimashita.
2. Tekitoo na shoosetsu o yomimashita.
3. Atarashii shoosetsu o yomimashita.
4. Iroiro na shoosetsu o yomimashita.

1. Takai tokei o kaimashita.
2. Kirei na tokei o kaimashita.
3. Iroiro na tokei o kaimashita.
4. Suteki na tokei o kaimashita.

1. Baka na koto o iimashita.
2. Warui koto o iimashita.
3. Hen na koto o iimashita.
4. Shitsurei na koto o iimashita.

Page 156
1. Biiru ga suki desu.
2. Tempura wa suki ja arimasen.
3. Tenisu ga kirai desu.
4. Tenisu ga totemo joozu desu.
5. Tenisu wa anmari joozu ja arimasen.

Page 157
6. Tempura wa anmari suki ja arimasen.
7. Tenisu ga joozu deshita.
8. Tenisu wa heta ja arimasen deshita.
9. Koohii wa kirai ja arimasen.
10. Tenisu ga heta desu.

1. Anata wa suupu ga suki desu ka?
2. Tomodachi wa gorufu ga joozu desu.
3. Haruko-san wa supeingo ga joozu ja arimasen.
4. Haha wa ryoori ga joozu desu.
5. Watashi wa anmari piano ga joozu ja arimasen.
6. Suzuki-san wa eigo ga joozu desu.
7. Chichi wa gorufu wa heta ja arimasen.

Page 158
1. heta na eigo 2. heta na gorufu
3. suki na keeki 4. joozu na tenisu
5. kirai na hito 6. suki na sushi
7. joozu na nihongo 8. kirai na suupu
9. heta na piano 10. suki na sensei

Page 159
1. Yamamoto-san wa sake ga suki deshoo.
2. (Sono) gakusei wa eigo ga joozu deshoo.
3. Ohta-san wa supeingo wa joozu ja nai deshoo.
4. Sensei wa kirai datta deshoo.
5. Taroo-kun wa (sono) terebi bangumi ga suki datta deshoo.

6. Haha wa (sono) keeki wa suki ja nai deshoo.
7. Sono hito wa piano wa joozu ja nakatta deshoo.
8. Takahashi-san wa (sono) tempura ga suki datta deshoo.

Page 160
1. benri ni 2. utsukushiku 3. anzen ni
4. genki ni 5. mezurashiku 6. tooku
7. suteki ni 8. rippa ni 9. fuben ni 10. tsuyoku

Page 161
1. (Sono) gakkoo wa anzen ni narimashita.
2. (Sono) gakkoo wa abunaku narimashita.
3. (Sono) heya wa kirei ni narimashita.
4. (Sono) heya wa kitanaku narimashita.
5. (Sono) resutoran wa shizuka ni narimashita.
6. (Sono) resutoran wa nigiyaka ni narimashita.
7. Fuben ni narimashita.
8. (Sono) gakusei wa kirei ni narimashita.
9. Genki ni narimashita.
10. (Sono) isha wa yuumei ni narimashita.

1. Kirei ni shite kudasai.
2. Benri ni shite kudasai.
3. Teinei ni shite kudasai.
4. Yasuku shite kudasai.
5. Raku ni shite kudasai.

Page 162
6. Hayaku shite kudasai.
7. Akaku shite kudasai.
8. Anzen ni shite kudasai.

1. The children played energetically.
2. The store clerk answered politely.
3. The doctor kindly examined him.
4. The student answered seriously.
5. He drove the car in a safe manner.
6. The town became modern.
7. The teacher taught well.
8. The flowers bloomed beautifully.

Page 163
1. hen de 2. suteki de 3. abunakute
4. akakute 5. baka de 6. modan de
7. iroiro de 8. fuben de

Page 164
9. teinei de 10. yasashikute

1. That building is very modern and beautiful.
2. (My) house was faraway and inconvenient.
3. That person is polite and refined.
4. Those sweets are beautiful and taste delicious.
5. The store is small and not at all convenient (in terms of location).
6. That person is stupid and inconsiderate (not considerate).
7. That restaurant was quiet and very delicious.
8. Japanese class is lively and interesting.

1. Sensei wa yasashikute shinsetsu desu.
2. (Sono) isha wa shinsetsu de joohin desu.
3. Ano ten-in wa wakakute kirei desu.
4. Uchi wa chikakute benri desu.
5. Ano gakkoo wa chiisakute anzen desu.

Page 165
1. (Sono) kooen wa kitanakute anzen ja arimasen.
2. (Sono) tekisuto wa kuwashikute muzukashikatta desu.
3. (Sono) hoteru wa atarashikute rippa deshita.
4. (Sono) mise wa chikakute benri desu.
5. (Sono) kooen wa shizuka de kirei desu.
6. Tomodachi wa hansamu de shinsetsu desu.
7. (Sono) toshokan wa ookikute benri desu.
8. (Sono) chiimu wa tsuyokute yuumei desu.

1. Ano eiga wa yuumei de omoshirokatta desu.

Page 166
2. Ano depaato wa benri de yoku ikimasu.
3. Ano sensei wa chotto hen de watashi wa anmari hanashimasen.
   That teacher is a little strange and I don't talk to her very much.
4. Ano isha wa shinsetsu de totemo suki desu.
   That doctor is kind and I like her very much.
5. Ano gakusei wa majime de itsumo benkyoo shimasu.
   That student is diligent and studies all the time.

6. Mise wa fuben de komarimashita.
   The stores were inconvenient, which was a problem.

Page 167
1. kirei ja nakute 2. kuroku nakute
3. anzen ja nakute 4. yuumei ja nakute
5. taisetsu ja nakute 6. majime ja nakute
7. yoku nakute 8. hima ja nakute
9. taikutsu ja nakute

Page 168
10. shitsurei ja nakute 11. suzushiku nakute
12. genki ja nakute 13. osoku nakute
14. furuku nakute 15. suteki ja nakute

1. Sono resutoran wa amari kirei ja nakute oishiku arimasen desu.
2. Sono konpyuuta wa amari atarashiku nakute osoi desu.
3. Sono seetaa wa amari takaku nakute suteki desu.
4. Sono hito wa amari shinsetsu ja nakute kowai desu.
5. Kono kuruma wa ookiku nakute fuben desu.

Sample answers
1. Amari oishiku nakute takai desu.

Page 169
2. Majime ja nakute suki ja arimasen.
3. Amari omoshiroku nakute suki ja arimasen.
4. Shinsetsu ja nakute suki ja arimasen.
5. Amari benri ja nakute suki ja arimasen.
6. Yasashiku nakute suki ja arimasen.
7. Teinei ja nakute suki ja arimasen.
8. Nigiyaka ja nakute suki ja arimasen.
9. Shizuka ja nakute suki ja arimasen.
10. Amari kirei ja nakute suki ja arimsen.

1. genki de 2. anzen de 3. raku ja nakute
4. shirokute 5. hansamu de
6. shinsetsu ja nakute 7. tookute

Page 170
8. chikaku nakute 9. suteki de
10. taisetsu de 11. nigiyaka ja nakute

12. benri ja nakute 13. majime de
14. tanoshiku nakute 15. modan ja nakute

Page 171
1. shirokute kirei na uchi
2. ookikute rippa na uchi
3. furukute yuumei na eiga

Page 172
4. ookikute kirei na daiya
5. majime de ii gakusei
6. shinsetsu de teinei na ten-in
7. furukute taisetsu na bonsai
8. mezurashikute kirei na hana
9. teinei de joohin na hito
10. wakakute genki na sensei
11. yasashikute tekitoo na hon
12. modan de kirei na biru
13. baka de taikutsu na hito
14. ookikute modan na machi
15. majime de hansa na isha

Sample answers
1. nigiyaka de omoshiroi tokoro
2. ookikute yuumei na daiya
3. ookikute rippa na iwa
4. hansamu de suteki na hito
5. atatakakute suki na seetaa
6. teinei de joohin na hito

Page 173
7. suzushikute kirei na kooen
8. furukute mazui tempura
9. gorufu ga heta de shitsurei na hito
10. majime de ii gakusei

Page 174
1. Is it all right if the coffee is not hot?

Page 175
2. Is it all right if the party is not lively?
3. Is it OK if the house is somewhat inconvenient.
4. Is it all right if the teacher is not famous?
5. It's fine if the rooms aren't clean.
6. Is it all right if the books are difficult?
7. The apartment doesn't have to be too modern.
8. Is it all right if his Japanese is poor?

9. Does it matter if the park is far?
10. Is it all right if the library is not quiet?

1. Anzen ja nakute mo ii desu ka?
2. Osokute mo ii desu ka?
3. (Sono) uchi wa modan ja nakute mo ii desu ka?
4. (Sono) eiga wa yuumei ja nakute mo ii.
5. Piano ga heta de mo kamaimasen.
6. Tenisu ga joozu ja nakute mo ii?
7. (Sono) densha ga hayaku nakute mo ii desu.
8. Toshokan wa shizuka ja nakute mo ii desu.
9. Hansamu ja nakute ii.
10. (Sono) heya wa kirei ja nakute mo kamaimasen ka?

Page 176
1. Libraries must be quiet.
2. The hotel has to be modern.
3. Beer has to be cold.
4. Students have to be diligent.
5. Store clerks have to be polite.
6. Nurses have to be kind.
7. Doctors can't be stupid.
8. Actresses have to be pretty.
9. Inconvenient houses are no good.
10. Planes have to be fast.

Page 177
1. Gakkoo wa anzen ja nakute wa ikemasen.
2. Gakkoo wa anzen ja nakute wa ikemasen.
3. Sushi wa atarashiku nakute wa ikemasen.
4. Kooen wa shizuka ja nakute wa ikemasen.
5. Kooen wa shizuka ja nakute wa ikemasen.
6. Yuubinkyoku wa fuben de wa ikemasen.
7. Yuubinkyoku wa fuben de wa ikemasen.
8. Yuubinkyoku wa benri ja nakute wa ikemasen.

1. Iie. Modan ja nakute wa ikemasen.
2. Hai. Yuumei ja nakute mo ii desu.
3. Iie. Shizuka ja nakute wa ikemasen.
4. Ee. Shiroku nakute wa ikemasen.
5. Iie. Kuwashiku nakute wa ikemasen.
6. Iie. Furukute wa ikemasen.

Page 178
7. Hai. Kirei ja nakute mo ii desu.
8. Hai. Tsumetaku nakute mo ii desu.

Page 179
1. I'll buy it even if it's old.
2. I'll buy it even if it's not cheap.
3. I'll go even if I'm not well.
4. Even if I have free time, I won't go.
5. I won't read the book even if it's famous.
6. I don't want that text even if it's good.
7. I'll go to the park even if it's dangerous.
8. I don't like that actress even if she's pretty.
9. Although that store is inconvenient, I always go there.
10. Even if it's bad, I will speak in Japanese.

Page 180
1. Kirei ja nakute mo kaimasu.
2. Atarashiku nakute mo kaimasu.
3. Raku ja nakute mo kaimasu.
4. Shizuka ja nakute mo ikimasu.
5. (Sono) resutoran wa shizuka ja nakute mo ikimasu.
6. Abunakute mo ikimasu.
7. Ano hito wa teinei ja nakute mo kikimasu.
8. (Sono) mise no ten-in wa teinei ja nakute mo kikimasu.
9. Ano hito wa shinsetsu ja nakute mo kikimasu.
10. (Sono) kangofu wa shinsetsu ja nakute mo kikimasu.
11. Daijoobu de mo kikimasu.
12. (Sono) kooen wa kirei de mo ikimasen.
13. Nihongo ga heta de mo hanashimasu.
14. (Sono) tekisuto wa muzukashite mo yomimasu.
15. Atama ga itaku nakute mo ikimasen.

Page 181
1. benri nara / provided it's convenient
2. joohin nara / provided they're refined
3. kitanakereba / if it's dirty
4. tookereba / if it's far
5. suteki nara / if it's attractive
6. majime nara / if you're diligent

Page 182
7. taisetsu nara / provided it's precious
8. yasukereba / provided it's cheap
9. rippa nara / provided they're fantastic
10. raku nara / provided they're comfortable

1. yoku nakereba
2. nigiyaka ja nakereba
3. taikutsu ja nakereba
4. ookiku nakereba
5. hansamu ja nakereba
6. atarashiku nakereba
7. genki ja nakereba
8. hima ja nakereba

Page 183
9. oishiku nakereba
10. mazuku nakereba
11. majime ja nakereba
12. hen ja nakereba

1. shizuka nara
2. nigiyaka ja nakereba
3. fuben nara
4. kitanakereba
5. kirei ja nakereba
6. hima ja nakereba
7. raku ja nakereba
8. hen nara
9. yuumei ja nakereba
10. akaku nakereba

Page 184
1. If the coffee shop is quiet, I'll go.
2. If the shoes are not comfortable, I won't buy them.
3. If the sushi doesn't taste good, I won't eat it.
4. If I am free tomorrow, I will go.
5. If I am busy, I won't go.
6. If I'm well, I'll go.
7. If the flowers are pretty, I'll buy them.
8. If the flowers are not pretty, I won't buy them.
9. If the dress isn't in good taste, I don't want it.
10. If the students are not serious, it's no good.

1. Kirei ja nakereba yoku arimasen.
2. (Sono) resutoran ga shizuka ja nakereba yoku arimasen.
3. (Sono) gakkoo ga fuben nara, yoku arimasen.
4. (Sono) kurasu ga taikutsu nara yoku arimasen.

Page 185
5. Gakusei ga majime ja nakereba yoku arimasen.
6. Kangofu ga shinsetsu ja nakereba yoku arimasen.
7. Biiru ga tsumetaku nakereba yoku arimsen.
8. Sensei ga teinei ja nakereba yoku arimasen.
9. Tenki ga warukereba yoku arimasen.
10. Kooen ga abunakereba yoku arimasen.

1. Seetaa ga kirei nara kaimasu.
2. Shoosetsu ga yuumei nara yomimasu.
3. E ga modan nara mimasu.
4. Hansamu nara aimasu.
5. Hima nara ikimasu.
6. Genki ja nakereba ikimasen.
7. Dame nara kaimasen.
8. Mizu ga tsumetakereba nomimasu.
9. Kutsu ga yasukereba irimasen.
10. Kuruma ga anzen nara unten shimasu.

Page 186
1. Rippa ja nakereba narimasen.
2. Modan ja nakereba narimasen.
3. Gakusei wa majime ja nakereba narimasen.
4. Kangofu wa shinsetsu ja nakereba narimasen.
5. Ten-in wa teinei ja nakereba narimasen.
6. Eki wa benri ja nakereba narimasen.
7. Gakkoo wa anzen ja nakereba narimasen.
8. Kodomo wa genki ja nakereba narimasen.
9. Kutsu wa suteki ja nakereba narimasen.
10. Shoosetsu wa yuumei ja nakereba narimasen.

Page 187
1. Kuruma wa akaku nakereba narimasen.
2. Isha wa shinsetsu ja nakereba narimasen.
3. Byooin wa chikaku nakereba narimasen.
4. Ten-in wa joohin ja nakereba narimasen.
5. Mise wa rippa ja nakereba narimasen.
6. Biru wa modan ja nakereba narimasen.
7. Suupu wa atsuku nakereba narimasen.
8. Wain wa tsumetaku nakereba narimasen.
9. Depaato wa benri ja nakereba narimasen.
10. Tekisuto wa tekitoo ja nakereba narimasen.

11. Niku wa atarashiku nakereba narimasen.
12. Densha wa hayaku nakereba narimasen.
13. Haiyuu wa hansamu ja nakereba narimasen
14. Heya wa kirei ja nakereba narimasen.
15. Eiga wa omoshiroku nakereba narimasen.

Page 188
1. modan ja nakute wa ikemasen
2. tsumetaku nakereba narimasen
3. anzen ja nakute wa ikemasen
4. genki ja nakereba narimasen
5. yoku nakute wa ikemasen
6. atarashiku nakereba narimasen
7. yasuku nakereba narimasen
8. majime ja nakereba narimasen
9. yuumei ja nakute wa ikemasen
10. benri ja nakereba narimasen
11. omoshiroku nakute wa ikemasen
12. shinsetsu ja nakute wa ikemasen

Page 189
1. Kirei ja nakereba narimasen ka?
2. Joohin ja nakute wa ikemasen ka
3. Atarashiku nakereba narimasen ka?
4. Benri ja nakute wa ikemasen ka?
5. Ookiku nakereba narimasen ka?
6. Modan ja nakute wa ikemasen ka?
7. Yasuku nakute wa ikemasen ka?
8. Majime ja nakute wa ikemasen ka?
9. Shinsetsu ja nakereba narimasen ka?
10. Suteki ja nakute wa ikemasen ka?

Page 190
1. Shitsurei datta soo desu.
2. Genki ja nakatta soo desu.
3. Fuben ja nakatta soo desu.
4. Shinsetsu datta soo desu.
5. Raku ja nakatta soo desu.
6. Suteki da soo desu.
7. Modan ja nai soo desu.
8. Hansamu da soo desu.
9. Kirei ja nai soo desu.
10. Tekitoo ja nakatta soo desu.

Page 191
11. Rippa datta soo desu.
12. Baka ja nai soo desu.
13. Yoku nai soo desu.

14. Hima da soo desu.
15. Yuumei datta soo desu.
16. Teinei ja nakatta soo desu.
17. Benri da soo desu.
18. Majime ja nai soo desu.
19. Taikutsu datta soo desu.
20. Baka ja nai soo desu.

1. I understand that the students at that college are all diligent.
2. I hear that that movie wasn't at all boring.
3. I understand that that movie actor was very handsome.
4. I understand that the bathroom at the station isn't very clean.
5. I hear that Tanaka's baby is very healthy.
6. I understand that his illness is fine.
7. I hear that his language was not very polite.
8. I understand that the nurses at this hospital are very kind.

Page 192

9. I understand that the Japanese textbook wasn't that appropriate.
10. I hear that kimonos aren't very comfortable.

1. Kono depaato no kutsu wa raku ja nai soo desu.
2. Ano hito no kotoba wa totemo teinei da soo desu.
3. Ano byooin no isha wa anmari shinsetsu ja nai soo desu.
4. Sono byooin wa totemo modan da soo desu.
5. Daigaku no kafeteria wa anmari kirei ja nai soo desu.
6. Sono kurasu wa totemo taikutsu datta soo desu.
7. Natsu no tenki wa itsumo hen datta soo desu.
8. Gakkoo no denwa wa dame da soo desu.
9. Doitsugo ga totemo joozu datta soo desu.
10. Nihon ryoori ga suki ja nai soo desu.
11. Anmari hima ja nai soo desu.
12. Tookyoo wa yoru totemo nigiyaka da soo desu.

Page 193

1. I understand that the shoes must be comfortable.
2. I understand that teachers must be strict.
3. I hear that he's not a very considerate person.
4. I understand that it's OK if it's not a quiet restaurant.
5. I hear that the colors have to be pretty.
6. I hear that the house doesn't have to be modern.
7. I understand that it's all right if the college isn't famous.

Page 194

1. Gakko wa benri ja nakereba naranai soo desu.
2. Hansamu na sensei da soo desu.
3. Seetaa wa kuroku nakereba naranai soo desu.
4. Resutoran wa shizuka de mo ii soo desu.
5. (Sono) heya wa kirei ja nakute wa ikemasen.
6. (Sono) shiken wa muzukashiku nakute mo ii soo desu.
7. Shinsetsu na hito ja nai soo desu.
8. Eigo ga joozu ja nakereba naranai soo desu.
9. Nihon ryoori ga suki da soo desu.
10. Haru wa atatakai soo desu.

Page 195

1. Nigiyakasoo desu.
2. Majimesoo desu.
3. Taikutsusoo desu.
4. Shinsetsusoo desu.

Page 196

5. Genkisoo desu.
6. Himasoo desu.
7. Taisetsusoo desu.
8. Joohinsoo desu.

1. Sensei wa shinsetsusoo desu.
2. Kono michi wa abunasoo desu.
3. Shiken wa yasashisoo desu.
4. Gakusei wa majimesoo desu.
5. Akachan wa totemo genkisoo desu.
6. (Kono) suutsu wa takasoo desu.
7. Kono mondai wa muzukashisoo desu.
8. (Sono) resutoran wa nigiyakasoo desu.

9. (Sono) toshokan w shizukasoo desu.

Page 197
10. (Sono) seetaa wa totemo rakusoo desu.
11. Korera no mise wa benrisoo desu.
12. Ano otoko no hito wa tsuyosoo desu.
13. Himasoo desu ne.
14. Gakusei wa taikutsusoo desu.
15. Ano gakkoo wa yosasoo desu.

1. genkisoo na akachan
2. oishisoo na keeki
3. majimesoo na kodomo
4. attakasoo na seetaa
5. himasoo na hito
6. tsumetasoo na hito
7. rakusoo na kutsu

Page 198
8. joohinsoo na onna no hito
9. benrisoo na jisho
10. muzukashisoo na mondai
11. shizukasoo na kissaten
12. shinsetsusoo na kangofu
13. kibishisoo na sensei
14. atarashisoo na yasai
15. tanoshisoo na paatii

1. Ano hito wa samusoo ni miemasu.
2. Sono sensei wa shinsetsusoo ni miemasu.
3. Tomodachi wa sabishisoo ni miemasu.
4. Ano seetaa wa atatakasoo ni miemasu.

Page 199
5. Isogashisoo ni miemasu.
6. Himasoo ni miemasu.
7. Biru wa shizukaso ni miemasu.
8. Niku wa atarashisoo ni miemasu.
9. Kono doresu wa takasoo ni miemasu.
10. Wakasoo ni miemasu.
11. (Sono) kutsu wa rakusoo ni miemasu.
12. Gakusei wa majimesoo ni miemasu.

Page 200
1. Akachan wa genki dattari genki ja nakattari shimasu.
2. Raku dattari raku ja nakattari shimasu.
3. Isha wa shinsetsu dattari shinsetsu ja nakattari shimasu.

4. Teinei dattari teinei ja nakattari shimasu.
5. Hima dattari hima ja nakattari shimasu.
6. Kurasu wa taikutsu dattari taikutsu ja nakattari shimasu.
7. Gakusei wa majime dattari majime ja nakattari shimasu.

Page 201
8. Shoosetsu wa yuumei dattari yuumei ja nakattari shimasu.

1. Teinei dattari shitsurei dattari shimasu.
2. Resutoran wa shizuka dattari nigiyaka dattari shimasu.
3. Kurasu wa taikutsu dattari tanoshikattari shimasu.
4. Sushi wa oishikattari mazukattari shimasu.
5. Machi wa modan dattari furukattari shimasu.
6. Gakusei wa eigo ga joozu dattari heta dattari shimasu.
7. Kudamono wa yokattari dame dattari shimasu.
8. Isogashikattari hima dattari shimasu.
9. Kirei dattari kitanakattari shimasu.
10. Urusakattari shizuka dattari shimasu.

1. Yokattari warukattari shimasu.
2. Isogashikattari hima dattari shimasu.

Page 202
3. Atarashikattari furukattari shimasu.
4. Omoshirokattari taikutsu dattari shimasu.
5. Nigiyaka dattari shizuka dattari shimasu.
6. Kirei dattari kitanakattari shimasu.
7. Shinsetsu dattari kibishikattari shimasu.
8. Joozu dattari heta dattari shimasu.

Page 203
1. Sono resutoran wa shizukasugimasu.
2. Himasugimasu.
3. Depaato no ten-in wa teineisugimasu.
4. Korera no biru wa modansugimasu.
5. Kono paatii wa nigiyakasugimasu.
6. Kono ongaku wa yuumeisugimasu.

1. (Sono) shiken wa muzukashisugimashita.
2. (Sono) eiga wa taikutsusugimashita.
3. Himasugimashita.

Page 204

4. Kono michi wa abunasugimasu.
5. Ano kuruma wa takasugimasu.
6. Majimesugimasu.
7. Ano uchi wa fubensugimasu.
8. Tookyoo wa nigiyaka sugimasu.

Page 205

1. I heard that Kyoto is pretty.
2. The teacher says that the students of this university are not diligent.
3. The teacher said that the text is not appropriate.

Page 206

4. He answered that that person was famous.
5. I think that Tom Cruise is handsome.
6. I heard that this park is not safe.
7. My friend says that the course was very boring.
8. I heard that the nurses at the hospital were not very kind.

1. Kono depaato no ten-in wa teinei ja nai to kikimashita.
2. Hima ja nai to tomodachi wa kotaemashita.
3. Eki wa benri da to kikimashita.
4. (Aono) chiimu wa tsuyoku nai to omoimasu.
5. (Sono) eki wa modan de benri da to kikimashita.
6. Totemo mazushii to ano hito wa kotaemashita.
7. Tookyoo no natsu wa atsui to tomodachi ga iimashita.
8. (Sono) eki wa totemo chikai to kikimashita.
9. Nyuu Yooku no tenki wa hen da to omoimasu.
10. Kimono wa raku ja nai to omoimasu.
11. Daigaku no kafeteria wa kitanakatta to kikimashita.
12. Sono byooin no isha wa totemo shinsetsu da to haha ga iimashita.

Page 207

13. Daijoobu da to kotaemashita.
14. Kono bonsai wa totemo taisetsu da to chichi ga itte imasu.

15. Ryooanji no niwa wa kirei da to kikimashita.
16. Kono kutsu wa raku ja nai to omoimasu.
17. Basu wa hayaku nai to chichi ga itte imasu.
18. (Sono) setsubi wa atarashiku nai to kikimashita.

Page 208

1. Ookina seetaa desu.
2. (Sono) seetaa wa ookiku nai.
3. Sono seetaa wa ookikatta desu.
4. Ooki na seeta deshita.
5. Ano seeta wa ookiku arimasen deshita.
6. Chiisa na inu o mimashita.
7. Chiisa na inu wa kawaii desu.
8. Watashi no inu wa chiisaku nai desu.

Page 209

9. Chiisa na machi desu.
10. Fuji-san wa ookina yama desu.
11. Tanaka-san wa ookina hito desu.
12. Ooki na mondai ja arimasen.

Page 210

1. Kooen wa nigiyaka na hoo ga ii desu.
2. Biru wa modan na hoo ga ii desu.
3. Bijutsukan wa furui hoo ga ii desu.
4. Sakana wa atarashii hoo ga ii desu.
5. Gakusei wa amari majime ja nai hoo ga ii desu.
6. Shigoto wa amari hima ja nai hoo ga ii desu.
7. Sensei wa kibishii hoo ga ii desu.
8. Heya wa kirei na hoo ga ii desu.

Page 211

9. Byooin wa chiisai hoo ga ii desu.
10. Kangofu wa shinsetsu na hoo ga ii desu.
11. Sarada wa tsumetai hoo ga ii desu.
12. E wa yuumei na hoo ga ii desu.

1. It's safer if there are a lot of people.
2. Sweaters are more comfortable if they're big.
3. Large flowers are prettier.
4. Lively parties are more interesting.
5. It's more convenient if the house is near.
6. Red dresses are more attractive.

7. It's more interesting if there are fewer students.
8. I prefer modern apartments.
9. New equipment is handier.
10. I prefer quiet restaurants.

Page 212

1. Eki wa chikai hoo ga benri desu.
2. Kutsu wa ookii hoo ga raku desu.
3. Inu wa chiisai hoo ga kawaii desu.
4. Biru wa modan na hoo ga kirei desu.
5. Uchi wa furui hoo ga omoshiroi desu.
6. Seetaa wa akai hoo ga suteki desu.
7. Paatii wa nigiyaka na hoo ga suki desu.
8. Setsubi wa atarashii hoo ga benri desu.
9. Kooen wa hito ga ooi hoo ga anzen desu.
10. Machi wa furui hoo ga yuumei desu.

Page 213

1. The more the flowers, the prettier they are.
2. The more serious the teacher, the better he is.
3. The more lively the party, the more interesting it is.
4. The nearer the stores, the more convenient they are.
5. The more modern the town, the cleaner it is.
6. The more handsome the actors, the better.
7. The more proficient your Japanese, the better.

Page 214

8. The older the shoes, the more comfortable they are.
9. The newer the facilities, the more convenient.
10. The older the wine, the more expensive it is.
11. The larger the car, the safer it is.
12. The bigger the eyes, the cuter it is.

1. kirei nara kirei na hodo
2. yuumei nara yuumei na hodo
3. modan nara modan na hodo
4. benri nara benri na hodo
5. hima nara hima na hodo
6. majime nara majime na hodo
7. suteki nara suteki na hodo

8. teinei nara teinei na hodo
9. anzen nara anzen na hodo
10. rippa nara rippa na hodo

Page 215

1. Suteki nara suteki na hodo ii desu.
2. Wain wa furukereba furui hodo takai desu.
3. Gakkoo wa anzen nara anzen na hodo ii desu.
4. Uchi wa benri nara benri na hodo ii desu.
5. Uchi wa ookikereba ookii hodo takai desu.
6. E wa modan nara modan na hodo omoshiroi desu.
7. Hima nara hima na hodo taikutsu desu.
8. Niku wa atarashikereba atarashii hodo oishii desu.
9. Bonsai wa chiisakereba chiisai hodo omoshiroi desu.
10. Inu wa ookikereba ookii hodo kawaii desu.
11. Biru wa modan nara modan na hodo kirei desu.
12. Mise wa tookereba tooi hodo fuben desu.
13. Doresu wa suteki nara suteki na hodo takai desu.
14. Kooen wa shizuka nara shizuka na hodo suki desu.
15. Eiga wa furukereba furui hodo omoshiroi desu.